# TWENTY-FOUR STORIES

BY

# HECTOR M. RODRIGUEZ

ISBN: 978-1-7355584-0-0

## Dedication

Dedicated to my family. Mateo for listening and seeing beyond his years, for Simon for being my friend of good spirits and peace, and Carole for being my rock. You my dearest wife don't take the cake; you are the cake.

# Acknowledgements

I AM FORTUNATE TO HAVE A GROUP OF CHARACTERS WHO HAVE been able and willing to listen to my stories. We meet once a week and share our offering with each other. We encourage each other and provide helpful comments. The group is fun, and their stories reflect fascinating glimpses of lives well lived. They are my dear friends and I thank them for reflective, insightful, and much appreciated commentaries. I want to acknowledge and thank Simon Johnson our astute and learned leader, Marion Whitney, Sarah Roome, Gerald van Belle, Johanna van Belle, Dave Horning, Sandy Horning, Adam Burlock, Victor Bracht, Kat Humby, Beth Brody, Ed Brody, Gene Stemmann, Jerri Austin Marler, Curt McCann, Deborah Wolf, Kay Novack, Marilyn Singh, Mike Mc Reynolds, Richard Raymond, Roberta Beck, Fred Hickman, Arona Rosegold and David Bickell. I would also like to thank Marie Stirk, my seasoned administrative support, for her help in getting the finishing touched completed. Thank you all for sharing the most valuable thing we have, our time.

# Prologue

I TOOK UP WRITING IN EARNEST ABOUT SIX YEARS AGO. I NEVER liked to write while growing up because I did not think I had anything to say. I listened a lot. Despite this, stories seemed to continually form in my mind, so eventually I decided to write them down. I started by writing a story about a man named Joe French. What happened to Joe French and the life he lived is a real mystery. It was my first attempt, and it got the ball rolling. Next, I took on a story about a journey with my son before delving into this collection. This book contains a variety of stories that provides a snapshot in time from the perspective of an aging boomer. I am average and typical in a lot of ways. I am cynical and sarcastic. I have had a good life. I am comfortable and intent on providing for the education of my family, a value you will see reflected in this collection. It is difficult to write. It is almost impossible to stay on task these days and the distractions keep pulling me away. A person needs to think deeply about the things they are going to say, write, and do. Time to have deep thoughts will help get it done. Some of the stories in this book are stand-alone chapters in books I have written and published or intend to publish. Several are works in progress. It's hard to say when something is truly finished. I have learned that it is futile to strive for perfection because you will never achieve it. No matter what you write, it will be subject to opinion both good and bad and will have at least one mistake. So, let's get on with it.

## Other books by Hector M. Rodriguez

*What Happened to Joe French?*
*The Path Taken*

# Contents

Acknowledgements.................................................v

Prologue .................................................... vii

Introduction...............................................1

Key West Impressions .........................................3

The Package................................................9

The Sisters ................................................20

Melissa Smith ..............................................26

April Fool's Day............................................56

The Trump Card............................................62

El Gallo...................................................66

Opening Day...............................................73

Elk Hunt 2021..............................................81

The Extraordinary Young Scout................................ 100

Angel .................................................... 108

The Chickens.............................................. 117

A Poem ........................................................................... 125

June 16, 1968 .................................................... 127

The Magician.................................................... 182

The Pioneers.................................................... 190

The Story of Agnes ........................................... 196

The Thinking Chair............................................ 207

The Three-Legged Chicken ............................................ 213

What We Take with Us ................................................. 216

When I Was a Kid ........................................... 222

The Bosses ...................................................... 228

The Horse and The Saxophone ...................................... 239

She .................................................................. 245

# Introduction

AS I SEND THIS COMPILATION OF STORIES TO THE PUBLISHER, I think back on the contents of this book. It is a collection of stories I wrote while living in Corvallis Oregon over the past several years. The stories are true for the most part. There are parts I take great license with and embellish beyond truth. I'll let you decide when the truth gets in the way of a good story. They reflect a life in the twenty-first century up to the twenty-second year of that century. There seemed to be some symmetry to the two and fours of our world. It is a time of drastic change for humans. Some stories are historical and leave little room for doubt. I share this humble offering as a snapshot in time. I want this to be reflective of our families, politics, humor, imagination and how we love. The stories run the gamut of subject matter. Keep an open mind and please, if nothing else enjoy each offering as a token of thanks for your time. Time is the most valuable commodity we have. As you read through the collection, you might find yourself hiding in one.

# Key West Impressions

HMRodriguez
Log Entry
Monday October 18, 2021—Key West FL.

Intriguing day. I headed to Key West for a three-night stay. I did not know what to expect. My imagined notion was a small quiet and sleepy settlement at the most southern point of the continental United States. It's where Hemingway lived for eight years and wrote some of his most well received stories. I will visit his house and polydactyl cats and perhaps get inspired to write more. I started to watch the sunset this evening. It was not as spectacular as I thought it would be. It was excruciatingly disappointing and every spot I chose was obstructed in some way with objects or crowds of people. The clouds were a homogeneous sullen gray. It looked like winter in Oregon but warm. I needed to find a better location. The main drag in Key West is Duval Street. For all intents and purposes, it's a drunken street crawl. Too many bars with wanna be guitar players banging out indecipherable songs over raunchy and abused Peavy concert speakers. Each bar competing with the bar next door for the international crowed of revelers. Each reveler with an iPhone in one hand, and a rum Mojito concoction in the other. Cigar smoke wafts out of the crowded restaurants with overpriced scallops basted in fake butter. Obesity is prevalent in both men and women, young and old. I wonder about the entertainment value of this place. It seems that if one is not drinking, smoking cigars, or eating, one is out of place. Men in flip flops, Tony Bahama tropical shirts made in Vietnam, and cargo shorts from Walmart troll the streets in a horny tango seeking the elusive one-night stand. Women, of all ages, dress to attract whatever they can, flirt and flitter about in lose fitting garb that beckons to any partner willing to engage in the sexual dance. Is it love or just a fling they seek? It's a sultry routine for this place. Some bars, it seems, are open around the clock willing to sell their alcoholic elixirs and potions to remove inhibitions and better judgement of crowds willing to pay for the hangover and shame the next day. And the criminals lurk, watching for the one who is stumbling, alone and unfortunately blinded by the salty air of adventure and blue waters of lust and chance of love and too much alcohol. The pickpockets pinch the wallets, and pry open the purses of those who are beyond their limits or perhaps too naïve to believe they too can be a victim.

As the evenings turn into dark star filled nights, the parties get louder and the drunk get drunker. The aroma of vomit on sidewalks blend with cigar smoke, and the local bartenders shake their heads saying yes and blend another cheap tequila margarita claiming it's the best in the Keys. With a heavy Cuban accent, they tell the tourists "It's the blend legendary Jimmy Buffet would drink," claiming it's the mix that lead to the song "Margaritaville". This is the blunt ball-peen hammer of island escapism. Escaping from what I wonder?

The older folks I see are probably my age. I am guessing they are at least in their sixties and probably older. We are the boomers. I wonder if I am really that old. We don't necessarily outnumber the younger crowd. But we are well represented with tanned skin, aching bones, and better judgement, I hope. We are the generation that has amassed the most wealth in the history of civilization. Of course, that statement can be debated as to what wealth truly is. Right now, good health is true wealth. What I see in places like Key West is a masquerade, an exorbitant display of consumerism that cries out a shallow howl of happiness. The problem I have is that I seem to endorse the folly. I do this subconsciously, unknowingly most of the time. Do I make the illusion come true because I have perhaps come to believe it? I find myself wondering if it's a catch-twenty-two. I look for the party and find it's one I don't really want to attend. But it's the only party I have an open invitation to. I reluctantly walk down the street looking for sane people, then realizing we are all crazy and filled with notion that this is real fun. It's interesting how our views change as we get older.

Some of the folks are wearing clothing they should perhaps reconsider. The neon orange spandex tube dress on a (cough) large-framed woman, can be an unsettling sight. Albeit beauty is truly in the eye of the beholder. But older potbellied men in micro speedo's always make me wince and wonder "What are they thinking?". At one point in time, I am sure my romantic notion of Key West existed. I think the draw of Hemingway in 1930's and his fishing triumphs, and the lure of the polydactyl cats, and simpler times intrigued me. One of the stories of the Hemingway House I recall was the addition of the pool to the property. It was the first pool in Key West and extravagantly expensive at the time. His wife Pauline built it. Hemingway was furious about it. But over time he grew to love it and built a six-foot brick wall around the entire perimeter house so he could swim in the nude.

The U.S. Coast Guard and U.S. Navy have been present since the early 1800's. The Coast Guard patrols the waters between the Florida Keys and Cuba. They keep a busy schedule with a constant influx of desperate people looking for a better way of life. It seems the immigrants are also looking for the illusion of wealth. They must have a strong burning desire to risk everything, including their lives to chase the dream. They come on boats bound together by hope and sail to far shores with the aid of empty fifty-five-gallon drums lashed together in makeshift boats. Over the years, thousands have paid thousands of dollars for a death at sea.

At 7:03pm I found a peaceful setting at The Fort Zachary State Park. It's open dawn to dust. I read a small tag on Google that said it's a place locals go. The sunset was a bit more willing to reveal its muted colors. The distant clouds were starting to grow and glow. Shades of red, purple, gray, pink, blue and yellow slowly emerged. Whispers of high clouds look like loose down, plucked from a great white goose. I only had a few minutes to capture pictures because the military police wanted visitors to leave by sundown. He went on to explain the Navy used the beach for night training. They drop Navy Seals about two miles offshore and the game is to get to the beach undetected and overtake the squad guarding the shores. Once night falls the game is on, and visitors are asked to exit quickly. The gates would be locked, and I may become a casualty if I am caught, so I was told. It sounded like fun to me. The guard did not think it was amusing. This area is unspoiled by the tourist frenzy several streets behind me. I hate being chased off by guards. I could have stayed on the beach for a long while. Progress as it is, can be a real pain in the ass.

If a writer knows enough about what he is writing about, he may omit things that he knows. The dignity of movement of an iceberg is due to only one ninth of it being above water.

Ernest Hemingway

# The Package

I WAS BOUNCING POOL BALLS OFF THE EDGES OF THE TABLE, calculating the direction the balls would travel and for how long. The pool table was in the center of Uncle David's Cantina. The plastic fake wood edges of the table were scarred by aged cigarette burns in several places. It cost 25 cents to play a game, but I played for free. The dirty pool balls had small chips. Several small tears and stains of spilled beer marred the green felt table-top, but it didn't seem to bother the patrons. Most of the customers were chipped and damaged in some way. They were all dirty and stained and scarred with the accidents of life, scared by years of circulation.

It was July 10, 1966. I watched the Orbiter 1 launch from Cape Canaveral on a black and white T.V. that day. The destination was the moon. I was almost 8 years old. I remember it was hot that day. It was always hot in July and I imagined horny toads running about carrying small umbrellas to garner some shade from the brutal sun. The South Texas humidity asphyxiated the air. It felt thick and heavy like wearing a wool winter coat in a sauna. A dust laden cobwebbed ceiling fan spun sluggishly in the center of the bar room. It didn't move much air.

Uncle David's Cantina was an old place with wooden floors, swinging bar room doors and rusted screens on the windows. It was the on the lower West-side of San Antonio, around the corner from our house on sixteenth street. It always smelled like popcorn, sawdust, beer, and sweat. My uncle served ice cold cans of Lone Star Beer, short brown bottles of Falstaff beer, Budweiser in cans, bottles of Coca-a-Cola and Fanta orange soda. He opened the place at noon and closed at midnight every day of the week, even Sundays. A large oval mirror hung in an ornate wooden frame over the bar. Uncle David said the mirror was broken during a gun fight years ago. A Mexican craftsman carefully sculpted its wooden frame of delicate roses decades earlier. The faces of customers sitting around appeared deeply carved with age. Their hands were calloused, dry, fossilized with arthritis, and dark by the sun.

There was a Wurlitzer jukebox set next to a corner of the room. It cost a nickel to play a song of choice. Stashed inside was an array of music including songs by Elvis Presley, Buddy Holly, Johnny Nash, Fats Domino,

Little Richard, Hank Williams, and Mexican ballads. An Otis Redding tune played through worn crackling speakers while a few dusty construction workers nursed their cold beers.

Uncle David was my after-school sitter. I hung out at the cantina during the summer. I liked my Uncle David's place. I was allowed to drink a coke a day. That was my pay. That and playing free pool to stay out of the way. Both my parents worked long hours and I'd typically spend my afternoons helping my uncle sweeping, stacking cases of empty bottles, and smashing empty cans. Once my chores were complete, I would pass the time by playing pool or reading comic books. One of my parents, usually my dad, came to get me in the evening or I heard him whistle and I would run home about dinnertime.

Mom worked at K-Mart in the clothing department. She made sure my older brother and I had good clothes. My dad worked at Sears and Roebucks selling Maytag washers and dryers, Frigidaire refrigerators and Kenmore stoves. "Major appliances every household needs," he said. He worked on commission. I didn't understand what commission was back then. They were nine to fivers and lucky to have steady jobs.

Joe French strolled into Uncle David's Cantina one day. It was the first time I remember seeing him. He and my uncle embraced with a strong hug. Joe bought everyone a round of drinks, including me. It was the first time I remember a stranger buying me a Coke. That was special and I liked Joe right off the bat. My Uncle called him a big spender, but Joe just shrugged the comment off. Joe and my uncle had a lot to talk about.

This was my earliest recollection of meeting Joe French. He was a mere thread of a man, wire thin and hard to forget. He became part of my early youth. I would be riding my bike and see Joe on a street corner, and he waved as though we were long-lost friends. Sometimes, he yelled out to get my attention and motioned me over.

We talked about all kinds of things. Joe frequently shook his head, laughed, and winked at me. I remember him saying, "Kid, you would not believe the shit I did when I was younger and how gullible people are. You keep peddling and try not to get into any trouble. But if you do, you better learn something from it." Those words have always lingered in my memory. Learn from your mistakes.

One time, Joe said he had serious thoughts of suicide. This was weighty conversation, a grown man talking to a kid about killing himself. I don't believe he ever got to that point, but if he did, he could have accomplished the task in numerous ways he said. He always carried a gun for one. It was a .38 Colt revolver, a "Police Positive" six shooter with mother of pearl handgrips. He said he bought in a pawnshop in Laredo. He kept the pistol strapped to his leg, beneath the knee, above the cuff of his creased slacks. I remember when he showed it to me. It was the first real gun I had ever seen. It looked like a toy until he let me hold it. It was heavy.

I don't think Joe worked a steady job. I would see him hanging out on the streets most of the time. I remember he carried a money clip and it was always full. He said he didn't owe anybody anything and he liked it that way. Within a few months, Joe became a regular in the neighborhood and moved into a room a few doors away from our home.

I remember Uncle David talking with his customers. They told dirty jokes, caught up on neighborhood gossip, talked about girlfriends and wives. Whenever he spoke with Joe, it was in a hushed voice. They tended to whisper to each other a lot. I never paid much attention to what was being said, but they seemed to be good friends.

"Give someone something free and they keep coming back for more, like stray cats." He said. Joe was friendly, wore strong cologne and a suit The cologne smelled like smoke from a campfire. One time, I watched Joe drink 151 proof rum shots one after the other and it didn't faze him. He just leaned to the left a little more than usual. Joe had a twitch in his left eye. It was a bit more pronounced when he drank. It was like a Turret's Syndrome reflex or tic. It was a curious trait. His left eye would begin to flutter for an instant then an involuntary wink, and the left side of his face would contort. It was as if he were telling you a secret and he was winking to make sure you knew he was telling you the truth. I would recognize that spasm anywhere.

Joe said he had been in prison. Fort Leavenworth, Kansas had been his home for a short while many years ago. He said it was the worst time of his life. Living in an 8 × 10 ft. cell was excruciating. He said it drove him crazy, until he escaped. When he talked to me about the escape, I found it hard to believe him. Some of his stories seemed too outlandish to be real.

He was odd, but over time I grew to like him. He became part of the neighborhood family. Joe played the alto sax, piano and sang songs on Saturday nights at my uncle's bar for a while. I remember he played lots of jazz and blues tunes. His voice was deep, smooth, and rich, like Otis Redding.

Joe was the first adult to talk to me like I wasn't a kid. He taught me how to swindle a few dollars from unsuspecting shop owners. It was my thirteenth birthday. Joe pulled a twenty-dollar bill from his money clip on which he had written the phrase "Happy Birthday from Uncle Joe" with a blue ink pen. He said, "I am going to go into the Woolworth store, purchase some socks and pay with this twenty-dollar bill. You wait here till I get back". A few minutes after he left the store he came back and said, "Go in and purchase some candy with this five-dollar bill. Before you walk out of the store, turn to the cashier, and complain you have been shortchanged. The cashier is going to say no you were not. Then you really start complaining and yelling you paid with a twenty-dollar bill your Uncle Joe had given you for your birthday. Tell the cashier the birthday wish was written on the bill. The cashier will look in the drawer and sure enough, there is a twenty-dollar bill with the birthday wish. You get to keep the cash." According to Joe, this was my birthday present. I did as he said. I got to keep most of the cash. This would be our secret. Joe said it worked almost every time, "Just don't go to the same store twice." he warned and only involve someone you totally trust. For some reason Joe trusted me. I later learned the real gift was the art of the swindle, not the cash. Joe had given me a lesson in the art of the scam.

He said, "Never tell anyone about the scam and always remember people are gullible. They will believe just about anything if you give them a reason to think it could be true. If it's in writing, it's even more believable. It called the power of the pen"

One day Joe vanished. He was gone without a word or trace, like a gentle gust of wind. Once I realized he was missing I asked around, but no one had seen him or heard anything. As a teenager where I grew up, that was a damn strange thing. I asked my uncle if he had heard anything; he shrugged his shoulders and said, "Some things are better left alone."

About a week after Joe disappeared, the police showed up. They investigated the area, searched his room, asked a few questions but never found a clue as to what happened. I often wondered what happened to Joe French. I wonder if Joe decided to move on to another city and live a productive normal life. I thought he may have got a job in another town, but I don't think I'll ever know for sure.

Joe had a way of making friends. People seemed to like him and trust him. Joe didn't appear to have any deep relationships like a girlfriend or any family; he never spoke about parents, brothers, or sisters. He was a loner. Uncle David seemed to be his closest at friend at the time. They had a special trust. It wasn't until many years later I found out how they met. It was in the Army in the 1950's. Joe French skipped across the surface of life, like a perfectly flat stone thrown across a still pond.

It was many years later my brother called and said he found a package addressed to me in the safe of my uncle's bar. My uncle must have forgotten about the package and after he died, the family cleaned out his office. The package was tucked on a shelf in the corner of a huge Lauer safe, where Uncle David kept everything of value because he didn't trust banks. The office was cluttered with stacks of invoices, random books, Playboy magazines, and travel brochures. It still smelled of stale beer, popcorn and cigarettes. A collection of old beer steins from Germany formed a ring around his office on shelves near the ceiling. The steins were covered with dust and cobwebs and had never moved. They were frozen in time. I'm not sure why my uncle had travel brochures; he never went anywhere I could remember.

I was living in Portland, Oregon when my brother told me about Uncle David dying. He was ninety-six and his health was failing over the last two years. I flew in for the funeral. After the service, my brother and I headed to the cantina. After having a beer, he handed me the package, I noted it felt surprisingly heavy. It was wrapped in plain brown paper and tied tight with several strands of kite string. The handwriting was faded, but you could tell it was addressed to me. As I cut the string with scissors the old brown wrapping paper crinkled and started to fall apart in my hands. Peeling back the wrap, I found an envelope was tucked into the top fold. It was evident it was not part of the original parcel but added later. It was addressed in simple handwriting to my uncle. The return address, written in pencil, was smeared, and faded. And I could see it said California. The postmark was dated January 24, 1972. It had an eight-cent stamp with an image of the multi-colored Olympic Game rings. It was from Joe French.

It was a short letter, and French said he was living in Beverly Hills Hotel at the time. He went on to say he was well, working as an extra in a movie called "Lady Sings the Blues", staying out of trouble, and had changed his name. He was thinking about trying to direct a picture in the next year or so. The letter ended with French inviting Uncle

David to come see him if he had the chance. The last line of the letter read, "You're a great friend. Joe"

As I continued to peel back the paper wrapping, memories of stilted and hushed conversations between my Uncle David and Joe came rushing back. An image came to mind of the two speaking quietly and then laughing. A slight waft of cigar smell wafted up once the wrapping of the package was removed. Under the wrapping was an array of old military standard forms, SF forms, in triplicate with carbon copy-paper attached. They were blank and yellowed with age. Under the small stack of forms was a cigar box, a Cohiba 1966 Edición Limitada wooden cigar box from Cuba. The box was interesting because of how intricate all the colorful labeling was. The box itself was a treasure.

As I continued unpacking the box a black and white photograph with two men in military uniforms standing with two attractive young women surfaced. A sign above the group read "Lebrun, Germany". I recognized the two men. One was Uncle David and the other looked like Joe French, tall and lanky. On the back was the date June 22, 1952. Under the photo, I found two dry Cohiba Cigars and Joe's gun, the .38 special with pearl handle grips. Under the cigars and pistol lay 4 bundles of $100 bills, each about one inch thick, neatly banded and taped tight. The bundles were packed snugly in the box like sardines in a tin. Under the cash, I found a tin box that held 33 gold ingots about one quarter inch thick, one-inch square. Each ingot had "U.S. Gov." stamped on it. I estimated the combined weight was about 2 pounds. My mind raced, two pounds, sixteen ounces to a pound, thirty-two ounces at $1200 per ounce; it was about $40K. Under the gold pieces, a key was taped to a 5 × 8 index card. It looked like a key to a safety deposit box. Printed on the index card was "First National Bank, New York City" and a nine-digit social security number 320-13-0022. Written in blue ink, under the number was my name.

*This is an excerpt from the novella an♦ mystery puzzle "What happene♦ to Joe French?"*

# The Sisters

I HAVE THREE GIRLS LIVING IN MY HOUSE. FAITH, CHARITY, AND Hope. They are wonderful roommates, clean, well groomed, pretty, and they provide constant entertainment. All three sing with extraordinary richness. They harmonize and work well together. I have enjoyed the music. I have enjoyed the diversity of their voices. I have played a guitar all my life. It started when I was a kid. I recall walking around in cowboy boots, sporting tattered blue jean cutoffs, a superman cape and strumming a wooden ukulele when the family was stationed at Fort Sam Houston in San Antonio, Texas. I was about six years old. I got a horse for Christmas that year. But that's another story. I was first introduced to a real guitar when I was attending St. Mary's University. A guy named Bill Wilson let me borrow one of his instruments. I had it a week or so and picked up a few chords. When I returned it, he said I should keep it. I did not keep it. I returned it but that experience ignited an interest in playing the guitar. I have never intentionally play for other people. It is a type of therapy for me. I have only owned a handful of guitars over my life. The first one I considered a worthy piece was a Guild orchestra guitar. It was a smaller construction, but she had a wonderfully deep resonating voice. She was a good instrument to work with. I would buy another, but they are rarer than I thought.

I sold that one ten or so years ago and eventually bought a Lyle from a pawnshop in Albany. It cost eighty dollars. I have spent a lot of time with Hope. That's her name. I liked her voice. I did not know it at the time, but the Lyle guitar was the subject of one of the most controversial lawsuits in instrument building and copy-writing business. The guitar was made in Japan but designed and distributed in the US by a man named Lyle Heater. Lyle went after the lower end market charging two hundred dollars per guitar. Back in 1960's and 70's, two hundred dollars was a good chunk of change for a guitar, but not outrageous. It did include a cheap case. Heater was selling the hell out of the guitar on the West coast, Los Angeles, Seattle, and Portland predominantly. His customers were the remnants of the booming hip-pie generation. They want to be Janice Joplins, Joan Baezs, Bob Dylans, Arlo Guthries, Neil Youngs, Crosby

21

Stills and Nash, and the Simon and Garfunkel crowd. Interestingly, the head piece of the Lyle guitar, called the headstock, looked amazingly like the headstock of the Gibson and Martin acoustic guitars. I believe Gibson owned Martin or vice versa. The Gibson Guitar Company filed a lawsuit against Heater's distribution company claiming the headstock design was proprietary and contributed significantly to the overall sound quality of the instruments. The battle went on for several years. Gibson, being the Goliath of the industry, prevailed and Heater had to stop selling his product in the US. The truth of the matter was the Lyle guitar was a great sounding instrument and Gibson didn't like the competition. The Lyle was made by a reputable company in Japan, and they used the best quality wood materials to build it. There is a visible element of beautiful craftsmanship in the construction of the instruments. Labor was cheap in Japan and Heater being a businessman took advantage of that. But the real test was the sound quality. Her voice was rich and deep and pure and alluring. The sound is truly unique to a Lyle. The one I own is fifty-two years old and she sings with aged refinement.

Charity came on the scene about three years ago. She was a local girl with a respectable background, broad hips produced from solid stock. Made with Guilds attention to strong bones, the guitar is firm and plays well with others. She came to me by way of Craigslist. I was thinking of replacing Hope when Charity found me. It takes good callouses to play her for long. She has heavy gage strings. For some reason, I did not spend as much time with her as I should have. I still treat her with respect. She is engaging and makes me appreciate her strong voice. You must hammer her strings hard to get her to cry. But she sounds rich and full when I get it right. She is young and needs more attention to build the pedigree she deserves.

Faith is the newcomer. I have been looking for faith all my life. To have faith gives a person hope. When a person has hope, they see others in need and provide charity. It is a cycle. I found Faith at an estate sale. She coyly sat in a dark corner in the basement of a large multi-story house. The house was in a heavy forested area and dampness was common, especially in the winter. It was a little cold, and I could tell she was uncomfortable. She looked unresponsive when I looked a little closer. I had seen such orphans in the past. I was sure several people noticed her. She did not look like a cheap girl. She had a long neck, graceful body, and well-appointed tuning jewelry. The headstock looked familiar except it read "CJMartin & Co. EST 1833" in script lettering. Hope sported the same boxy headstock design. I picked her up gently and strummed the slightly worn steel strings. She was out of tune. I noted she had onboard electronics, a place to plug in an amplifier and a built-in tuner. The tuner was not working as far as I could tell. Upon further inspection, I noted some of the soundbox molding was separating on both the top and bottom. I thought that was due to the damp conditions she was living in. It was not too serious, but eventually would need to be repaired. There was also a small crack on the side of the soundbox. It was hard to see, but I could tell she had been dropped. Probably more than once. Her previous relationships must have been rocky and unsettling with arguments and ill words and careless handling. Probably too much drinking or such. She was lonely and not cherished as she wanted to be. One of the estate sale attendants pointed out she came with her own traveling case and stand. I was told the case was made from alligator hide. It was not a cheap traveling valise. Despite flaws I noted, I made an honest attempt to take her home, but it was not appealing enough. But it was not appealing enough. I left my name and number if she changed her mind. I left feeling remorse, a bit of sadness thinking I should have offered more. She needed a warm home. Two days after the sale ended, I received a call from the owner of Faith. If I was still interested, he was willing to accept my offer.

My three girls all hold a special place in my heart. They are so different but similar in many ways. They keep each other company, but more importantly, they keep me company. It feels like I have always had Faith. It feels good to have faith. It feels like a new sense of commitment. She sings with a confident and seasoned voice for being the young one of the threesomes. I am spending more time with Hope, Charity, and Faith. I am hopeful my relationship with the sisters will last a long time.

# Melissa Smith

SPOTTED MELISSA SMITH AT A YARD SALE IN KAMLOOPS, British Columbia the summer of 1994. I could tell she was young, maybe ten or eleven. By the clothing she was wearing I could not tell if she was rich or poor, not that it mattered. It's been said only the rich can afford to wear rags. She looked sad, revealing a stern compassionate expression with piercing brown eyes. Her eyes followed me as I looked over the mélange of used household items scattered about the lawn. Her untidy and oily black hair was messy, as though she may have found the ritual of combing hair unnecessary, or she may not have owned a comb. She was wearing a frayed red wool shawl, wrapped around a deep forest green dress turned up at the bottom. The beige material backing the hem was exposed. Her white slip was slightly exposed. She wore no shoes and it looked like she was seated at the opening of a cave. I was to learn, it was the entrance to Smith's Pocket, her father's mine. It was fall and golden maple leaves were scattered around her feet and about the yard, rustling in the crisp western breeze when I first noticed her. As the seasons of my life passed, I would learn much of M'Liss and her life. I would cherish her with all my heart.

I bought the painting that crisp fall day in Kamloops B.C. I bought it because I liked the subject. It was also an original oil by a long-lost painter. It houses paintings by Picasso, Van Gogh, Degas, and many others in their impressive collection. About twenty-five years ago, I started to do research into the painting of M'Liss after I received a call from my mom. Mom had seen a print of the young girl in the painting. She'd seen it in the McNay Art Institute in San Antonio, Texas. The McNay is an art museum and cultural events venue. It houses paintings by Picasso, Van Gough, Degas, and many others in their impressive collection. She wrote down the name of the company listed on the bottom of the print and sent it to me, "Leighton Brothers, London".

The painting titled "M'Liss," was done by an Englishman named Edwin Long. As I continued my investigation, I contacted a person known as Dorimant, an art appraiser from London I met over the internet. I learned "M'Liss" was the heroine of Bret Harte's novelette of the same name and was painted in 1872, towards the end of the gold rush.

It was exhibited at the Royal Academy Exhibition the next year. Dorimant went on to say aside from the Leighton Brothers' print, a copy of which is in the British Museum of Art, the picture was also reproduced in the Illustrated London News in 1875. Although owned by George Hearst in 1887, its present whereabouts was unknown and rumored to have been destroyed by fire. The report from Long's critics said the portrait possessed the depth of the Mona Lisa with a wild west twist. When Long painted her, he was mesmerized and captivated with her rough and yet graceful appearance. When he finished the initial raw depiction, he considered it his best piece. He felt drawn to the image and wrote in his journal there was something special about Melissa. He was in his early twenties when he discovered the girl. The painting would haunt him the rest of his life.

Bret Harte's stories of the wild gold rush days were read by thousands of people all over the world. His story of Melissa Smith would eventually be turned into a 1920's motion picture. At some point, the painting of Melissa Smith was acquired by George Hurst. He kept it in Hurst Castle residence in California. Then a rumor of a fire sometime in the past tells several pieces of the collection were destroyed. It could have been true, and the Hurst family specifically would collect insurance monies to help sustain the period lifestyle. The trail went cold until the painting surfaced at a yard sale in Kamloops B.C.

Her father was named Washoe Smith. He was a prospector and miner during the California gold rush. He discovered gold in the Sierra Nevada range in the northeast region of the new state. His claim was far up a canyon and was one of the best producing claims in the region. It was dubbed "Smith's Pocket". Other lucky prospectors found gold in the area and a small mining camp quickly flourished in the general vicinity of the Red Mountain. Washoe Smith's pocket of gold made him rich, for a while. He found gold nuggets with milky white quartz in deep narrow crevasses that were once ancient creek beds. Some cleaned nuggets weighting more than twenty ounces each.

He staked his claim in late 1859. The pocket produced over five thousand dollars in gold within a week of discovery. Smith was living large and spending much of his new fortune on mining equipment and drinking and gambling in both town's saloons. In about 1863, Smith fathered the child. He was not able to care for the infant nor did he have the desire. The child's mother disappeared shortly after the birth. No reason was given, but rumor had it she moved on to another mining town, a good distance away. But that is not what happened, that was just the rumor. The night she left she felt a break in her heart. She knew she would come back for Melissa. The infant was passed around from family to family until she was able to beg for herself. The juvenile was undisciplined, unkempt, and considered wild and uncontrollable. By the time she was eight, she was on her own, wandering the dirt streets of Red Mountain. Everyone knew her, most taking pity on the unruly, skinny and dirty child. Ten years later her mother would return.

Smith needed to work his claim and a mine was no place for a young girl. He was around thirty years old when he struck it rich. When the gold started to play out Smith worried about his young daughter. He was dead at age thirty-nine. When Melissa discovered the body, he was gripping his pistol and had a hole through his heart. The death was ruled a suicide, but it wasn't a suicide. She knew it and so did the resident physician of Red Mountain, Dr. Clapp. Clapp was also the coroner and dentist. The fact was Washoe Smith found another promising pocket of the precious metal. Smith visited Dr. Clapp earlier that day and told him. Smith paid his bill with ample diggings. He thanked the doctor for being so kind and watching out for his daughter and teaching her to read and write. Smith told the doctor things were going to better for Melissa. The doctor wanted to believe him, but he knew better.

The last time I saw the painting of M'Liss pieces of paint were beginning to fleck off the bottom left corner. The signature cannot be clearly read. There is a one-inch tear on the center left of the canvas. It just missed the red wool shawl M'Liss wears. The wooden stretcher and canvas show signs of stained age and adventure. When portrait painters of the time worked, they did sketches of their subjects and use the sketches to paint the final. They would do the final in their studio. It could take a while to complete a portrait. The piece was done by someone who cared about their work, with diligence and grace but in a bit of a hurry. Long was young and developing his skills in the 1870s. I have Googled some of his later work. Some sold for serious money at auction. I have often wondered how this particular painting found its way to a yard sale. The painting I purchased may well be the original. Using field supplies, in a hurried environment of the gold rush frenzy, Long captures the very essence of life in a rude, cruel and unforgiving time in a simple yet elegant portrait of this young orphan girl. But he was in a hurry.

The story of M'Liss is a twisted path of adventure and luck, albeit sometimes bad luck. The tale is set in a time of little law and many desperate people and continues today. What was so intriguing about this young girl that would bring an English portrait painter and a successful writer to Red Mountain to tell her story? Harte's narrative about this young girl is a peek into life of a homeless and orphaned child during the California gold rush. A child with grit, determination and cunning borne out of desperation. It is carefully crafted. He wrote how people found M'Liss as an incorrigible girl yet captivating.

According to Harte, her fierce, ungovernable disposition, her mad tantrums, and lawless character were only superficial. She was lonely and lacked any sense of family. But that would change as she matured into a woman of strong character. The way Harte writes the story he was intrigued with her disregard for authority. Melissa spoke her mind; it was all she knew to do. She did not understand the concept of rules necessarily. Harte was the original owner of the painting. Long painted it at his request. I don't know if Long was paid or not. The painting brought her to life beyond the hovel of Red Mountain. Harte grew fond of her over the years, but she probably did not realize how much he cared about her. They were from different cuts of society. He treasured the painting and only sold it out of desperation, needing money to pay off debts. She was his real-life Huckleberry Finn of the west. She was his Tom Sawyer of the Gold Fields. Harte held a special love for the child and then young woman. He wanted to help her until circumstances changed their lives forever. Harte was married and had three children. His wife was not well. She suffered from what could be described as severe bi-polar disorder. Harte spent too much time with her.

M'Liss, Brett Harte, Edwin Long, Dr. Clapp, Bill Miner, Washoe Smith and the town of Red Mountain are intertwined as part of the gold rush mystique. There is an abundance of information from that period. All of these players have a common interest at one point in time— Melissa Smith. Harte was a good writer and published numerous articles and stories of the gold rush days. The one titled *The Luck of the Roaring Camp an◆ Other Tales* holds the story of the idyl of Red Mountain, M'Liss Smith. Harte was a contemporary of Mark Twain. Early on they collaborated and co-authored a play called "Ah Sin" in 1874. They eventually had a falling out. Twain claimed Harte was "unethical, a thief, a liar, a cheater, a swindler, a snob, a sot, a sponge, a coward, a Jeremy Diddler, and a pool gambler." Twain repeatedly referred to Harte as "The Immortal Bilk".

One of the reasons they had a falling out was due to the story of Huckleberry Finn and Tom Sawyer and how it paralleled the story of M'Liss. The story was written before the other two stories. Speculation says Twain stole the idea from Harte and developed the Huck Finn and Tom Sawyer personalities. The concept of a smart youth heroine or hero that over comes challenges and wins in the end. Twain vehemently denied that accusation and that is when the fracture in their relationship started. Twain claimed he had the idea first and he thought having a girl heroine was preposterous. Nevertheless, Bret Harte went on to write poetry, give lectures, give book reviews, editorials, write plays, magazine sketches and authored numerous stories about the gold rush. He was editor for the Atlantic Monthly for a short period and started the Californian Magazine. He wrote like his life depended on it. He did however, go through some hard times as did many people in the 1800's. At one point, Harte stopped writing the story to assure the reader it was fiction. It was not fiction however, but rather a compelling yet veiled attempt to tell of M'Liss, the circumstances of her life, the untimely demise of her father Washoe and small fortune in gold lost. It was the epitome of the California gold rush adventure told through the eyes of a young prolific writer. A rag to riches story with murder, revenge, and mystery. Eventually Harte leaves Red Mountain and moves on to write other stories, but always harbors a curiosity and fondness for Melissa Smith.

The story pieces together the life of Melissa Smith as she lived as an independent woman of the gold rush era and how she avenged the death of her father. The story also tells how Edwin Long's masterpiece ended up in a Kamloops, British Columbia yard sale one hundred fifty years later. And finally, the story of how Brett Harte lost a small fortune as he chased the story and admiration of M'Liss Smith around Red Mountain, California.

# Red Mountain

The town of Red Mountain was two hundred miles east of Sacramento. At the time Harte arrived the town consisted of two hundred-sixty-eight permanent residence, two saloons, two hotels, one boarding house, one house of ill repute, two general stores, a well-managed livery stable with a blacksmith, a stagecoach office with one telegraph line, a presbyterian church with a parsonage in disrepair, several rustic dilapidated but livable cabins, and a jail. Several cabins were painted white and looked like quartz outcropping against the iron rich surrounding landscape. The town was spread apart in such a fashion, when some-one stepped off the stagecoach, they often wondered which way the center of town was.

A permanent structure consisted of a structure stand-ing longer than a year. Tents, either round or square did not count. Livable cabins of either stone or wood, with four walls and a roof flanked the main street on both sides, some sitting hundreds of yards back over undulating foothills that grew gentler to the south and steeper to the north. The church was the only structure that showed any care was given regularly. A lone oak tree in front of the building provided shade during the summer family picnics. Next to the church was a small cemetery. Harte noticed the mound of fresh dirt and a simple wooden cross. A grossly carved wooden plank lashed to the cross bore the name

W. Smith. On the top of the cross was a simple, delicately woven wild-flower wreath. The doctor's house was across the street from the church, next to the cemetery. It was an unusual occurrence when the stagecoach came into town. People wandered into the streets to see who the newcomers were, thinking one might have been a family member. Most of the travelers and prospectors came from horseback or on foot.

The gold claims were north of the town in the foothills and then deeper into the Serra Nevada mountains. Long canyons fingered up the rugged slopes. Miners used the abundant Pondarosa pines as timbers to shore up walls of their diggings. Some of the claims were dotted with black openings of tunnels burrowed into ancient riverbanks and canyon walls chasing veins of the yellow metal. Some miners were developing hydro-mining techniques to wash the gold laden soils into tumblers and rockers. Crude aqueduct systems were spaghettied over the hills in several locations. There were hundreds of working claims.

Miners consisted of native Indians, Swedes, Germans, Mexicans, Englishmen, American blacks, Chilenos, Frenchmen, and mulattos. They tended to keep to themselves until trusting relationships developed. The Mexican American War had recently ended, and tensions were high between several groups. If someone did not outright own a claim, they probably worked for someone who did. Theft of tools and provisions was common. Workers not getting paid was a regular occurrence and lead to occasional fights and killings. The early on, workers were paid six dollars a week. They lived at the mine site in canvas wall tents. Common practice was to construct the floors with split pine timbers. Sanitary conditions were not optimal and disease such as dysentery was common. There would be a common source of water, a seasonal creek flowing through the middle of the canyon.

## The Queen of Harte

The harsh alkaline dust was kicked up by the six-horse team pulling the Slum Galion Stageline coach as it entered the town of Red Mountain. Everything, the passengers, horses and onlookers carried a fine layer of the reddish dust. It was August 9, 1848. A warm and dry afternoon in the Sierra Nevadas. As Brett Harte stepped off the couch and surveyed the sparse looking town, he wondered who or what his next story could be. A ratty, skinny, and disheveled looking little girl held out her hand and said, "Change"?

Heart searched is vest pocket.

"Here." And placed quarter in her smallish dirty palm. It's all he could find.

She looked at the coin and said, "Thank you."

"I'm Harte and who are you?" he responded.

"Melissa. What are you doing here?" she asked meekly.

"I am here to write a story about the gold folk are finding. Do you know who I might talk to? Who is finding gold?"

"Mr. Harte, this is Red Mountain and I really can't tell you who is finding gold."

She thought about this. She hesitated.

"If you buy me a soda, I'll tell you what I know."

Harte looked at the young girl. He looked across the street at a fresh painted sign "Lopez-Cantina-Cold Beer", thinking a cold beer sure sounded good. "That sounds fair Melissa. Let's go."

As she started to cross the street, Harte grabbed his worn leather valis and followed her.

There were four men in various states of drunkenness lingered inside the Cantina, one of the towns two saloons. The floors were wooden, and a long brass pole anchored to the floor supported several patrons' dusty worn boots as they bent over the bar. Several spittoons were placed along the bottom of the bar, full of a toxic mixture of spit and vomit from those who drank too much. The barkeeper looked at Melissa as she hopped up on a wooden stood.

"Lemonade Mr. Chuck. This man Harte is treating me." She said smiling.

The bartender looked sharply at Harte and nodded with a shrug of his shoulders in agreement as Harte asked for a beer. "Two bits." He said, "I cut her off after two drinks. If she has too many, she gets sick. What brings you to town, Harte?"

Harte started to explain, he was starting a magazine called "The Californian" and writing stories about the gol-drush. He glanced at Melissa saying the young girl sounds interesting. The bartender said "She is interesting. She is the town orphan. He father committed suicide about two weeks ago."

Harte took a heavy pull of his beer and started to ask Melissa questions.

"I've been here all my life." She said, "I know everybody. And they all know me. My father found gold up the valley." She drank her lemonade quickly. Harte cocked his head and started writing. She told him she didn't know her mother. Her father said her mother worked at the saloon but left after she was born. She said would come back for her. Melissa went on to talk about Dr. Clapp and how he was looking out for. So was the town preacher, Mr. Cole.

"I'll take another if you don't mind." as she tilted the glass up and gulped the last swig, Harte started thinking, it was perfect.

Harte place two more bits on the bar, pointing to the empty glass and his mug as he gulped the last of his beer.

"This town is all I know, and it has secrets." She spoke in a hushed voice.

"How did your father die?" he asked.

"When I found him over on the side of the road, he was holding his gun in his right hand, tightly and he had a hole in his heart."

Harte thought about this and kept writing.

"Why aren't you in school?" asked Harte.

"I can read and write a little."

"Where do you live?"

"In my father's cabin." With that she took a long gulp of the lemonade. "Thank you."

"Melissa, I need a story about this area. I'll be here a week maybe a little longer. Can we talk more?"

She hesitated and said "Sure."

As she jumped off the stool and heads outside, Harte noticed a small pistol beneath her shawl.

⸎

He looked at the barkeep and ordered another beer. As it was being poured, he asked about the young girl. The bartender told Harte the town folks kept an eye on her as best they could. He went on to say Washoe Smith was as good a father as he could have been given the circumstances. He worked his claims most time, now that he was dead, no one was sure what was going to happened to Melissa. She was a fixture in the town. No one came or went without Melissa knowing about it. She was protective of the people in the town that helped raise her and they were protective of her. Except for another young girl named Clytemnestra. "They are enemies," explained the barkeeper. It was a rivalry thing. She was not afraid to protect herself. She could be as mean as a wounded mountain lion. On the other hand, she was alone and needed protection. She had a good heart and helped where she could.

Harte inquired about other amenities the town offered. After a short discussion, he downed his beer and crossed the street to National Hotel. A few dust-covered men stood outside the bar looking like greenhorns down on their luck. Harte figured they had not found the strike they wanted.

It was sometime during this period Harte decided to write the story of Melissa, the idyl of Red Mountain. Here was a girl who could be the heroine of the gold fields. He would make her story part of his collection. It was brilliant but sad. This would be the story of an orphan in the wild west that could hold her own ground.

He decided to send a wire to a young painter he knew named Edwin Long from England and invited him to the frontier do a portrait of Melissa. Harte knew Long was in San Franciso working. With the new money gold was bringing in and the excitement of the times, Harte knew people wanted adventure stories. The wild west was still stoking the flames of imagination all over the world. Harte needed to get publicity for his magazine and having Long do a painting would be a good way to start. A picture was always a good thing to have.

As Harte was leaving the saloon, he saw the young girl crossing the street headed to the National Hotel. He watched her as she cautiously dashed across the dusty road. He pondered "What would become of this child's life? What will she do?"

He followed the girl into the National and found the clerk, a well-dressed Indian woman behind a wooden desk. Her name was Sally Bean, and she had an extremally large nose to the point of being remarkably odd. After speaking with her, he secured a room and put his belongings away. He headed back to the lobby with pen and pad in hand, still dusty from the road. He asked where the doctor's office was, Hart apparently was nursing a painful carbuncle on his upper leg. He walked out into the late afternoon sun. He was getting hungry.

"Where ya going Mr. Harte?" It was Melissa. She was standing on the front porch of the hotel surveying the dirt street.

"I'm going get some dinner. Are you hungry?"

She was but too proud to say so. As Harte looked at her, he noted her skin was dark from the sun. She was exotic, wild looking, feral in a way.

"Can I write down what you say? I want to write a story about you." asked Harte.

"I don't know Mr. Harte; I can tell you I have the claims that belonged to my father. Thar's what Dr. Clapp tells me. I'm not exactly sure what I am going to do with them. Daddy always told me there was more gold. He just knew it."

Harte thought about this for a few minutes. He was a writer, not a miner. But this young girl needed help. Perhaps he could help.

"Melissa, I am not a miner, but maybe we can help each other. This would make a great story. I might be able to help you sell the claims."

She thought about that for a minute. She wasn't that sure she could trust him. She remained silent and then said, "The Cantina has good food."

Harte looked down at the dirty, skinny little child and smiled.

" Melissa, let's go eat." He stretched out his hand.

M'Liss eyed him. She reached out her small brown hand and shook his.

"Let's go."

Harte thought about sending a wire to Long. It would take him at least two weeks if not longer to get to Red Mountain.

## Edwin Longsdon Long

Edwin Long was staying with Georgia Hearst and her family near the center of San Francisco. He was commissioned to paint a portrait of her. That portrait being completed, Long was enjoyed various sights while waiting for the next patron to arrive. He was planning to return to England in the fall. Long spent several evenings walking near the docks watching sailing ships come and go. It seemed a bit colder than usual, the fog was constant. It reminded him of London. He could hear yelling in the distance, commands bringing ships safely into the docks. As he started his walk back to the Hearst mansion, he passed a gangly group of men with cloth bags pitched over their shoulders. Prospectors he thought, headed into the gold fields scattered in California and maybe the Yukon. Most were young and ambitious; some were old men still harboring hopes and dreams of striking it rich. Many of the travelers never returned home but died in their quest for riches.

Long was in his mid-twenties. He had taken his ability to paint seriously. Early in his life he was sent to study at the British Museum of Art in London. He met Harte a few years earlier while visiting England. Harte came from a well-connected and educated family. His father, a wealth Jewish merchant, was starting an investment stock exchange in New York City with several other merchants. This was to be the beginning of the New York

Stock Exchange. Long and Harte ran in the same circle of wealthy families and became friends with a common interest of exploration and adventure. When Long received the wire earlier in the day, he was intrigued.

"Edwin-come to Red Mountain. East of Sacramento. Need you to paint Melissa Smith. Opportunities abound. Please acknowledge—Harte"

Long must have felt Harte was on to something. He was intrigued by the Californian magazine and opportunities to showcase his work. At the same time, he was considering mining investments for his family and a trip to the Red Mountain area may have opportunities to investigate. He decided to go to see his friend before leaving for home. Long sent a return wire to Harte indicating he was on his way. He returned to the mansion packed a bedroll, small suitcase, his two-shot derringer, a satchel with paints and brushes and told Georgia of his plan and when he would expect to return. He went to the livery, selected a fit horse, threw an English saddle on the beast and started out for Sacramento, his first major destination along the way.

The road to Sacramento was well traveled. The fields were open sage and prairie grass for the most part. This was good range. Cattlemen began claiming sections of this country quickly because it was so temperate and feed so abundant. Every now and then Long spotted a rustic cabin carved into the horizon. The fields concealed a natural dark, rich soil and water appeared to flow abundantly. The native Americans were not too aggressive, although Long read about skirmishes every now and then. The third night Long camped near a family of cattle ranchers. They told him about recent Indian attacks north of Sacramento indicating a safer route. They also talked to Long about the change in weather and how snow was seen in the peaks of the Sierra Nevada mountains to the north. It was early for snow.

His time traveling through Sacramento was brief, but entertaining. He visited the Eagle Theater, the first public theater in California.

## Washoe Smith

Washoe Smith's claim was up a canyon five miles due north of the town of Red Mountain. The area was covered in tall timber. Boulders of all sizes hid beneath a thin forest covering of pine needles and a dark soil veneer. Gold in this region was imbedded in the cracks and crevasses of the bedrock beneath the soil covering. Sometimes, decent sized three-to-six-ounce nuggets could be found in the topsoil. But those kinds of easy pickings were far and few between. Smith's first find was easy pickings. His claim was significant. He drew a lot of attention that first year and hired several workers to help with his claim.

That year winter came early, and freezing temperatures solidified the creek in early September. Smith cut back his operation and spent the winter enjoying his new-found wealth in town. He built a small cabin close to town in hopes of attracting a wife although the selection of eligible women in the mining town was slim. Washoe did attract the attention of the prostitutes and became a regular. They knew he had money. Melissa's mother apparently worked in one of the town's premier establishments called the Empire Hotel and Saloon. She was young and got pregnant, claiming Washoe was the father. The rumors and speculation inferred Smith was the father, but proof was only what one said. Melissa's birth was not recorded on a certificate or such. The only record was a hand-written note in Smith's mining journal. Washoe must have felt some responsibility for the child because he tended to her needs the best he could. He felt sorry for the child and he did have the means to help her. He supported her out of the goodness of his heart.

Smith worked his claim for close to 7 years. He was able to purchase equipment and pay his claim fees. Early on the claim was dubbed "Smith's Pocket", because everything he found went right into his pocket and out again.

The last twenty-four hours of Smith 's life was exhausting. He was working his claim, swinging his pickaxe. It would reverberate with a sharp high pitched "ping" at impact all day long. The walls of the pit consisted of decomposing quartz mingled with flaky mica that reflected here and there with the candlelight lantern. He was working hard to break down the boulders blocking his way and widening the walls in the pit. When he looked hard at the chunks of granite, he could see flecks of gold. The ore was good, and he was able to carefully extract the larger flecks of pure gold with his fingers. The light was fading, and he needed another candle soon.

He was thinking about finding another pocket when a large section of the wall fell away exposing a rich ten-inch-wide vein of gold. Then his miners lamp candle went out. He threw his pickaxe down and turned to the dark shaft. He knew the way out, even in the pitch dark. He had been over the terrain a thousand times. He was excited, pondering how he was going to get the gold out and if this was the motherlode. As he made his way in the dark, he kept thinking he found the vein again. It was that ever-elusive vein of gold. He knew they existed. What he didn't realize was how large the vein actually was. It would be years before the large mining companies would bring in mega-ton capacity crushers, steam powered mechanical beasts, and remove hundreds of tons of rock to get to the end of the vein. All Washoe knew, in the back of his mind, he needed to find gold and settle his debts. He knew he needed to take the gold he could extract and save it for Melissa too. Washoe knew what he needed to do.

Once he made the climb to the opening of his mine the fresh cool air hit him. It felt good. The stars were bright, and he headed to the water bucket. After a few good sips, he sat down and thought of his life. The Serra Nevada fall breeze floated through the canyon and cooled his sweaty skin. He could not understand why his luck was so bad. He sold most of his usable equipment and that money almost was gone. He grabbed some dried ham from a worn burlap sack. It tasted good, especially the salt. He reached for his bottle of whisky and took a long sip. It warmed him up inside. He then grabbed his sleeping roll deciding not to start a fire. He rolled out his bed and closed his eyes. "Tomorrow." he thought. "Tomorrow I'll dig out a lode". He thought about his daughter. He wished he could be sure she was okay. His heart ached knowing he squandered so much of his small fortune. Eventually sleep overtook him.

Early the next morning, Smith piled back into the mine and removed several large nuggets of pure gold. By late afternoon he was on his way to town. He grabbed his pistol, a colt six shooter and put it in his burlap sack. Then he reached for his leather pouch of gold he extracted and pushed it deep in the side of his pocket of his jacket. The mine was hidden from view due to a large oak tree's branch broke in such a way it balanced with a see-saw balancing result. It poised in such a way a small child could easily and effectively move the branch, thus exposing the entrance to the mine. Smith climbed down the rocky face, and into the stream bed, gingerly balancing on talus debris of unstable rocks as he made his way. The water was at a trickling pace in late fall. But he knew in the spring the stream turned into a raging flood, sweeping away tumblers, sluiced, crudely constructed water flumes, tents, and people. The previous year two miners died by drowning in the torrent flow. It normally took three hours to walk to the Empire Hotel and Saloon in the middle of Red Mountain. Most of the going was on the main trail used by miners and their work beasts. Test holes from prospectors littered the grounds in all directions. Horses, mules, and men all had to be careful when coming and going otherwise they may trip and fall resulting in broken bones.

Two days later Melissa found her father dead, off the road in a small gully. His burlap sack was missing as was his small leather pouch of gold diggings. Besides his pistol, he had nothing except a small, ripped page of paper from his mining journal in his vest pocket. At first glance it looked inconsequential. She knew he was robbed and shot. The piece of paper was not important to who killed Smith. But Melissa recognized it and knew it was important. It was from her father's journal. The claim rules of the community required miners to keep a journal of mining activity or their claim could be lost to another. If a prospector did not document his claim and what work was done, it could be taken away by any other person. The rules relating to staking a claim were sometimes reflective of Darwin's theory of survival of the fittest. First, there were no State laws on claiming ground for mining. This was early in the pioneering days and each community was permitted to construct their own rules. Typically, a claim was an area forty by forty feet. The miner would then "stake-off" the area putting a notice on wooden stakes indicating who's claim it was and the date. The miner may choose not to work the claim but was obliged to renew it in ten days with the local claim registry, usually maintained by a State Land Regulator. Without doing so, any other person has the right to "jump-it". Some miners hired laborers to work a claim, paying them a predetermined wage. Washoe had workers at one time. But he recently could not afford to pay his bills. He owed one forty dollars. His name was Chaco, and he was desperate. Washoe kept notes religiously of all his mining activity, including who he owed money to. He knew he owed a few men some money and he needed to pay them, but Chaco was mean. He never like owing people money. On the piece of paper in his pocket when Melissa found him were the coordinates of a new claim. Melissa ran down the hill to get Dr. Clapp.

Melissa summoned the doctor to help with her father, the doctor engaged the help of several townsmen. When they arrived at the location, about 2 miles out of town, the doctor noted Smith was clutching his pistol. That observation did not set well. It was not in agreement with a suicide of this nature.

## A Woman of Easy Virtue?

Melissa's mother was named Marion Witte. She was a prostitute. Many women followed men to the gold fields looking for support in a husband or mining themselves. A lot of gold was being produced and money was flowing like water in the creeks in some places. The establishments that made most of the money included the services industries. Hotels prospered, as did the saloons, blacksmiths, doctors, lawyers, bankers, mining equipment suppliers, and whorehouses. It is somewhat certain a young girl does not aspire to work in a bordello, but circumstances being what they were, many women found threads of security in such employment. This was the case for Marion. She was a young attractive woman with an eye on Washoe. His pockets were deep. His mine produced thousands of dollars, he was a hard worker and unmarried.

Once she realized she was pregnant, she was uncertain what to do. In the end she had the child. Being young and unable to support the baby, she decided to abandon the child and left town. This was a decision she would regret for the rest of her short life. One might ask how a mother could leave her infant child. Again, circumstances of the time made for tough choices.

# The Painting

Long could see the glow of Red Mountain as the sun was setting. It was late September and the leaves on maple trees were turning bright colors and falling. A crisp north wind slinked down the long canyons. When he arrived, his first stop was the Empire Hotel. He asked the clerk for Harte's room. He found Harte writing at a fevered pace. It was a welcomed reunion. He explained to Long they needed to find M'Liss. That was what the townspeople called her. Harte gathered his coat and writing tools and went to look for her with a tired Long in tow. She was not in her usual places, the patio of the hotel or the doctor's office. At the saloon he learned she had gone up to her father's mine. She did that on occasion, disappear for a few days and work on her father's claim. Harte and Long would saddle up two horses and head to the mine in the morning. They did not know exactly where it was, but the directions indicated they could get into the general area and find it most likely.

The next morning was bright and clear. Fall was in the air. As they rode the five miles up the long-twisted canyon, Harte talked with Long about the story he was writing. He told of the death of her father, where he was killed, and about Melissa and how strong a young girl she was. Although she was an orphan, she had manners and could read, write, and do simple math. Harte felt he wanted to adopt her but knew he could not. He was already married at the time and had two children. His wife was an extremely jealous woman to the point of driving Harte away for months on end. It was all he could do to tolerate her. He felt she may have had an uncurable mental condition. Was this a bipolar disorder? This of course was kept quiet, and it appeared to many Harte abandoned his family over the years. This included his onetime friend Samuel Clements.

## The Call—June 2014

When the email the came in, I thought it was junk. It was a Tuesday afternoon. Dorimant's story conveyed the painting had surfaced back in 1908. I immediately printed the email reading again. It surfaced in an article in a newspaper in London saying a reward was being offered for the location and safe return of the "M'Liss" painted by Edwin Longden Long. There was an address for Leighton Brothers Printing Company in London.

I googled the company and found it was no longer in business. The brothers stopped making prints in the late 1880s.

I was not sure if the painting was once truly considered the Mona Lisa of the West. But at the same time, I could not seem to put this story to bed. I needed to contact an art historian and get the painting looked at for restoration purposes. I also want to get my art evaluated and probably insured. I have never been a serious art collector, but my mother taught me to keep an eye out for several things. Old art was one of those things. She took me with her as she walked up and down the rows at Bussey's Flea Market on the northside of San Antonio. She knew where the good dealers were. Occasionally a painting would show up at one of the flea market booths, mostly still life rendering. She would buy a few of them over the years. I am sure some of her paintings have increased significantly in value. I recalled the first time she saw M'Liss. She offered me one thousand dollars on the spot. My mother never parted with that kind of money without good cause. I did not sell it. But oddly enough, a few years later she came across a print of the painting and that was when my relationship with Melissa Smith truly began.

HMRodriguez
Log Entry
April 1, 2022 (April Fool's Day)
Corvallis, Oregon

# April Fool's Day

*(Note: This is mostly true, except for the parts that aren't.)*

M FATHER WAS BORN ON APRIL FOOL'S DAY. I THINK people that are born on April Fool's Day are infused with the ability and desire to created misery, havoc, confusion, and condemnation among friends and family. My dad was like that. He would pull off practical jokes. Jokes that were supposed to be funny. For the most part they were funny, but some were mean. According to Webster's online definition of practical joke, it is a trick played on someone to make them look foolish and confused. It's usually at the expense of the pride or ego of others. Most jokes are of a lighthearted nature and a good laugh and time will usually erase any ill feelings. There are some jokes my dad played I have never forgotten. I'll let you be the judge as to if they were good or bad or even practical for that matter.

My dad was an attorney and a member of the Texas Bar Association for over fifty years. He was an eagle scout and knew when and where he could cross the line, so to speak. The law did apply to him, but he knew when and where he could bend it just a little. He enjoyed having a good laugh. On this occasion, he was living in El Paso working for Texas Social Service Commission as legal counsel. He had an executive style office with a few staff secretaries. The secretaries were efficient, good-natured people. One that worked with my dad was named O'Thatisa Fullnelson. She was a top notch and a truly nice person. For reason only known to my dad, he obtained some letterhead from one of his fraternity brothers at the State Attorney General's office and wrote O'Thatisa the following letter.

"Dear Mrs. Fullnelson,

This letter is to inform you that your house has been confiscated by the State of Texas due to unpaid taxes. You will have about ninety days to pay your taxes or vacate the property.

Respectfully,
Ann Richards
Attorney General
State of Texas"

Dad placed the letter in an envelope from the AG's office, so it looked real. He also put it in an interagency mailing pouch that gave it an even more urgent sense. He went to the mail room to have it delivered. When Mrs. Fullnelson retrieved the mail the next day and opened the letter, she was horrorstruck. She had never been late with her taxes; she always paid all her bills on time. She started hyperventilating, immediately called her husband trying to explain the letter. She was in high orbit right now talking in a loud exasperated voice, almost crying. The other secretaries in the office of cubicles were on their feet looking in her direction and the other young attorneys in the office were on high alert, curious as what all the ruckus was. My dad was watching from his office door, I can't imagine what was going through his head. He may have been wondering what his next move was going to be. Apparently, he had not thought through the possible chain of events. This wasn't looking like the fun he was planning, or was it? I wonder if he had thought out the long-term consequences of his joke.

My dad decided to call off the prank as O'Thatisa hung up the phone. I understand her husband went into cardiac arrest shortly after the call. My dad explained it was a joke. A poor joke he thought would have been a funny prank. Eventually, he calmed O'Thatisa down and told her he was the one who sent the letter. He explained he thought everyone was too serious in the office and a little fun would go a long way to build up team spirit, or "Espree de corps." He told her he was sorry, and everything eventually calmed down. Mr. Fullnelson did not go into cardia arrest. But he was upset at the time but was fine. They had a good laugh and did grow a little closer as time went by. What I think the real purpose of that chain of events shows is what a little out of the box humor can do. For one thing, it made a memorable story. O'Thatisa re-told that story several times over the years and each time, she seemed to laugh harder and smile a little brighter. She told the story again at my dad's funeral and thanked him for the memories.

Christmas, 1966, was another occasion he was spurred into joker mode, and it involved me, and I wanted a horse. I was the atypical kind third grade kid at the time and my dyslexia kept me at the bottom of my class despite what I thought was a pretty good effort. I could run like the wind but academics were not my thing. What seven-year-old kid, raised on John Wayne, Clint Eastwood, Gunsmoke, The Lone Ranger, Lassie, Bonza, Rawhide and the Wild Wild West didn't want a horse? I wasn't any good at this schoolwork stuff, surly a horse would make life better. I was a pest of a kid and asked over and over for a horse and a side kick dog. I did not care what kind of dog, but it couldn't be a poodle. Cowboys don't own poodles.

I had it all planned out and told my mom and dad I would keep my horse in the basement of our government issued quarters located on Infantry Post. Infantry Post was a housing area at Fort Sam Houston. Dad was stationed there several times during his twenty-nine-year military career. I used to know it well. My army brat buddies, and I would run wild through the military warehouses, barracks, parade grounds, and officers' quarters. We would climb on static displays of Sherman tanks and 40mm artillery pieces positioned all over the post. I would occasionally find myself at the Boots and Saddle Riding Club, the horse stables. The army always keep a small detachment of period Calvary for parades and ceremonies. It also offered horse boarding; a privilege reserved for General Staff. It was also a sweet assignment if you're a cowboy.

Christmas morning, after my brother and sister and I completed opening our gifts, my dad looks at me and says, "Son, there is one more gift for you. It's tied up out front." I looked at my brother and sister, they have big grins on their faces. I sauntered to the door in my best Clint Eastwood imitation, knowing what I was getting. I was getting a horse. I knew it. I opened the door and looked out. It was winter and the trees looked like skinned naked bones and it was ice cold for a Texas winter. I ran out into the yard but could not find the beast. "He must have gotten off his lead!" I yelled. My dad yelled back, "He is tied to the front door!"

I turned around and tied to the front door was my horse. It stick-horse with the plastic red and white cartoon drawing of a horse head with a cheesy grin and a yellow yarn mane. The pole was red. I was heart broke, and my family had a good laugh. So, was this a good joke? I think it was kind of mean. Although I look back on it now and it's probably a good thing, I did not get a horse. If I would have, this would be a totally different story. I get reminded of the story on frequent occasion. My siblings can be relentless. Did this joke meet the intent of a good practical joke?

My dad also told untrue stories. Not exactly lies but tall tales I took for truth. In a way, it strengthened my perspective on gullibility. I wonder if such stories can be considered practical jokes. I recall my dad telling me about the spaghetti bush and the evil Bo weevil infestation of 1968. As the story goes, he told me there was a tremendous plague in Italy of a mysterious insect that decimated the spaghetti bush. I had to do my part in managing the crisis and my dad convinced me to plant strands uncooked spaghetti on end, three to a hole. The holes had to be one foot deep, and I planted six noodle plants. I watered the plot for two weeks hoping to see sprots of the firm noodles. Sure enough, two weeks later, to the day, in the afternoon when I returned from school, I found packages of noodles from Cesar's Italian Kitchen right where I planted the uncooked stuff. My older brother and sister shook their heads and looked the other way. We enjoyed noodles for dinner that evening, and no one asked where the noodles came from.

# The Trump Card

USUALLY DON'T WRITE ABOUT POLITICS. IT ONLY LEADS TO debate, and and some are not worth the time or energy. Some people are master debaters. I am not a master debater. I am a writer. I have been somewhat confused lately with respect to our current political situation. First off, I have always voted a democratic heavy ticket. My dad was also a democrat and if I did not vote democratic, he would kick my ass. What I can tell you is we did talk politics. He was a lawyer and a master debater. I know there has always been dissention between political parties because that what political parties do. They are groups of people that interpret laws and rules in certain ways and tend to agree with each other. They feel they are fair in their personal interpretations and perspectives.

My confusion lies with how to interpret what President Trump is doing. Either he brilliant or as crazy as a loon. Let's assume for the sake of this argument, he falls smack dab in the middle. He is very smart and at the same time, a few cards shy of a full deck. We are not all perfect. I want to lay out a potential scenario for the Trump Card. Let's consider he knows exactly what he is doing. First and foremost, he understands the media and how to manipulate several forms of media to his advantage. He understands the reach of social media and what it takes to keep it focused on him. He has given the media exactly what they want, something to write and talk about. Okay so he is controlling the media. It's a Svengali-like move. It's misdirection. "Hey, everyone, look at me" while the other hand is doing the magic. It's a Three Card Monty in this case. Trump knows the Three Card Monty; he is from New York City, for crying out loud. What is next? He is building his dynasty. He understands power and money. Is he the best power broker and money manager? Nope. Remember, he falls smack dab in the middle of the pack, he is very smart, but he does have priorities and we can rest assured it's not you and me. I would imagine his top priority is his family. Isn't that yours?

So, let's step out of today and think about long term planning and impacts. Trump has set into motion a hoard of possible outcomes due to his tenure as President of the US. He has members of his family infiltrating the US

Government in the highest echelons. Trump Jr. has the highest levels of security clearance, so does Ivanka. So do several other family members. They are learning the ropes. They are observing how the government machine works. They are asking the question, "How can the family benefit from the machine?" Right now, I imagine the lieutenants from the Trump dynasty are in uber-learning mode. This is a long-term game. I wonder what they are telling young Barron Trump. Are they telling him he could be President?

I watched some of the Republican Convention. I believe in an equal voice and that means listening to other perspectives and interpretations. While I was watching, I kept wondering and asking myself what do so many people see in the Trump philosophy? What am I missing? I have been consumed over the last three and a half years with media reports on the gaffs, misguided reports, and outrageous statements. Am I watching one hand while the other does the magic? The press is ready to pounce. Anything that will garner views and excite Twitter is a green light. Even if it's true. I must say Trump has not been kind to the media. It must be part of his plan. The noise level stuff does not bother him. He is thinking long term. In fact, he is creating what can be described as a legacy. The legacy will not be counted in votes but rather long-term impacts to the relative strength of his dynasty. His dynasty will be around for a long time. Is this the next Ming dynasty? I don't know. I will not be around to find out.

The "It's about me!" slice of the American population is siding right up to Trump whether they know it or not. We all want the American dream. We want to be able to provide for our families and be kind to our friends. We all want to be able to speak freely, worship our image of God. Above all we want to be treated fairly, especially with respect to the law. We want our country to be strong and we want to feel protected. We want our homes to be heated and water to be clean. We want to feel safe and heard.

I think that's the Trump Card. He is running the country like a Three Card Monty game. While we are watching the cards drop on the table to guess where the red ace is, he is picking our pocket and building the walls of his dynasty. He is making sure we are heard. Just look at the media and what we are consuming including Corona Virus, Chinese sanctions, election fraud, Postal Service disruption (let's face it, the Postal Service has been running for over two century's and suddenly, it's not?). I wish us all well, regardless of the outcome of future elections and I am still confused. God Bless America.

# El Gallo

I REMEMBER MY GRANDFATHER GRIPPING MY HAND FIRMLY AS we approached the old barn nestled back on a line of scraggily mesquite trees and prickly pear cactus in Hondo Texas. The earth was baked and dusty and I noticed dried cow patties randomly littered across the ground; no horses or cattle were in sight. A corral with several boards missing made a pen that held wild mustangs was now empty. A fence post held a neatly coiled rope with a familiar lasso loop. It was early evening, and the hard South Texas sun was withdrawing its last rays of light from another blistering day. The moon had gone into hiding behind distant billowing red clouds that faked hints of rain. Several vaqueros in dirty chaps and large brim hats were standing near a half empty wooden watering trough; their muffled voices uttering colorful slang Spanish curse words describing the women and beers they longed for. The dust was thick and brown and gentle puffs of clouds rose as I watched the measured steps of other men also walking towards the ancient barn.

There seemed to be an uncomfortable exhilaration in the air as we stepped into the dimly lit structure. Several oil lanterns were hung on bent, rusty nails that protruded from aged wooden beams that crisscrossed the low ceiling, casting dark shadows across the dusty floor. Spanish chatter was erupting as men gripped wads of dollar bills tightly in their dirty, soiled, and calloused hands. It was money, real money, hard earned cash. Men were handing bills back and forth, and back again. It was more money than I had ever seen in my young seven years of life. As grandfather pushed and moved us forward, I felt anxious and excited with anticipation of what was happening. We pressed through the crowd that smelled of pungent sour sweat. The smell was of men of labor, tough work and difficult lives. The men were baked brown from the sun; they were the color of the earth that surrounded them.

As we reached a row of large wooden crates on one edge of the room, grandfather lifted me up and set me on a post, and said "espera aqui", wait here. I watched him closely as he made his way back across the room searching for someone. As I watched, he pulled something out of his pocket. I saw glint of gold as he started to argue with a stranger, but the stranger brushed off the dialogue and turned away. Grandfather moved on to another man and started to argue, showing a small gold locket dangling from a gold chain. The new stranger grabbed the locket and opened it up; as he closed it they shook hands. My grandfather made his way back, giving me a tentative smile. The room became more and more crowded with men yelling and arguing and passing money back and forth. I curiously watched, not understanding the commotion or intensity of the event unfolding before my eyes as the dust rose in billowing folds. Grandfather sat next to me on a crate. I had a king's seat and was able to look out over all the commotion in the room from my perch on the post.

Another man arrived and started to talk. I could make out some of the conversation about one of the roosters that was going to be fighting. His name was El Gallo del Diablo, rooster of the devil. It was rumored that the rooster was stolen from the village of Salinas in deep Mexico and had been smuggled across the Rio Grande by a man named Chavez. The man also said that this rooster had never been beaten. Grandfather shook his head. He heard about El Gallo del Diablo, but that the reigning champion of this area was quite good. The champion was named El Maestro and had never been beaten either. El Maestro had fought 100 fights and had left 10 of his challengers dead in the sand; Grandfather was sure he would be the winner in this battle.

As I sat and listened, the roar of the room became deafening. Men were yelling and swearing and pushing and shoving and sweating. Dollar bills were everywhere, trading dirty hands and then disappearing into pockets. After a short while, I saw four men with two large crates moving thru the crowd. The crates were non-descript, but I could tell they were important by the way the crowd of men parted to make room. As the crowd started to quiet, the men placed the crates at opposite sides of the large circular arena about 20 feet apart. The crate holding El Maestro was placed right next to the post I was sitting on and I was able to peer in and see a magnificent rooster. His tail feathers stood tall and proud with a litany of reds, blues, yellows and greens. His comb was deep red and scarred from previous battles and I sensed the rooster had no fear. I watched his eyes darting and bouncing from target to target, looking for his challenger through the slats of the crate. His beak was cracked and chipped, yet his voice screamed in a screeching pensiveness in anticipation of the battle to come. He was the largest rooster I ever saw. El Maestro had two broken sagging wings and scars with missing feathers on his breast and his spurs were tied back like double-edged daggers poised to strike. He was a warrior, a gladiator of the ring, proud of his many victories and ready for the next battle.

From the other side of the ring, I could hear El Gallo del Diablo crowing his call to battle. As I watched, men exploded in excitement. Money started to change hands again, arguments ensued, and hands were clasped in agreement. A signal was given, and the cage doors were flung open. The two roosters charged to the center of the ring in a flurry of dust as their wings beat winds of fiery intimidation towards the other. El Gallo del Diablo was magnificent. He was completely black, including his comb, hackle, cape, back, tail feathers, shanks, spurs, claws, and toes. He was missing one eye and the other had a scar across the eyelid, which caused him to cock his head in a sideways position, looking for an opening to strike. His spurs were long and looked like Roman spear points at the ready. El Gallo del Diablo looked evil and wicked, like a rooster the devil would have kept for himself.

I watched in stunned amazement as the roosters attacked each other and rose far above the dirt floor, squawking screams of torment and torture, gnashing at each other as spurs and beaks dealt targeted blows. Feathers flew in chaos as the ring of men cheered and screamed and flailed arms in madding anger as each rooster traded blow after blow. As the roosters rose far into the air they would separate and fall in heaps of feathers and flesh only to charge again and again and again, daggers and spear points pirouetting to inflict fatal blows.

As the crowd roared in twisted excitement, I saw my grandfather caught up in the frenzy of the battle. His once soft voice was now yelling in a tormented and anguished primordial fevered pitch of passion. It was a moment I would never forget; it eviscerated my image of a calm, sensitive and tender wise man. I saw him in a way that changed me forever. I saw a man of war and torture and hurt and pain. He was relishing the battle, perhaps recalling his youth and the fevered emotions of a young desperado fighting with Emiliano Zapata during the Mexican revolution many years ago.

As the roosters fought, I was mesmerized not so much by the battle, but rather the excitement and hunger of the crowd. I became one of the cheering masses as the birds continued to rise far above the ring, ensnaring the crowd into the blood lust duet of death. I started to cheer as my grandfather did because I wanted to be one with him. I felt confused but wanted to be part of the moment, and I was. I was experiencing a feeling I had never known. As the roosters rose into the dust filled air El Maestro sunk a gash into the shiny breast of El Diablo and El Diablo buried a spear deep into the leg of El Maestro and then into his neck. As they fell back to the earth, El Maestro could not stand, his leg was gashed and broken and bleeding. He could not regain his fighting stance. El Maestro hobbled frantically spinning in circles, looking for his balance and leg. As he gyrated, El Diablo rose majestically and drove his spear like spurs into the neck and head of El Maestro burying him in the blood caked dirt floor of the arena again and again and again until he was spent. It was done. The room was silent.

El Gallo del Diablo was collected and put back in his crate to heal and begin the journey to the next battle. El Maestro was collected to be thrown into a trash heap outside of the barn, to rot and decay in the hot Texas sun. Grandfather grabbed my hand as we walked back to the old pickup truck in silence. Once in the truck, he told me that the locket he had lost was his mother's and it contained the only picture he had of her. He said he was so ashamed that he had lost it and he cried. It had always brought him good fortune. As we drove home in silence the old truck rattled and swayed through the dry Texas night. I saw heat lightning far off in the distance. It looked like burning alcohol flashing across the dark sky. I hoped it would rain.

# Opening Day

THE HUNT THIS PAST SEASON WAS REMARKABLE IN SO MANY ways and at the same time unremarkable. I found myself in Ukiah, Oregon for an elk hunt in early November 2019. I have a buddy I hunt with. I call him 2NN. His name is Glenn with 2 "N's", not one. He is a good guy, a bit older than I and part Native American from Northern California. We have hunted together for the past 18 years. It's good to have a hunting buddy. We have a routine, developed after a few years of making mistakes, getting on each other's nerves, and learning to appreciate each other's talents. He is a great cook, and I don't mind washing the dishes.

This year, like several years in the past, we alternate who gets to choose where we hunt on a particular day. In preparation of this hunt, we scouted an area and 2NN had a hankering to explore it. He had a feeling. He always has a feeling. It did not matter to me as I knew there were many elk in this part of the country. There are really thousands of elk in this region. It's prime habitat. It's a matter of convergence. Convergence is an interesting phenomenon. It's the matter of two or more events or things coming together to evolve into a culminating outcome. A writer's workshop is an example of a reoccurring convergence. Many things must happen for the group to meet. One of the primary things one must do is write something, and then make the effort to converge, hence a convergence. But I digress.

We arrived at our primary hunt location about eight miles up Butcher-Knife Ridge. It's named Butcher-Knife because you better bring one with you. It has that many elk. 2NN decided he was going to head up a forest service road to the north and hunt it on opening day. He had a feeling. He always has a feeling. I told him I was going south. I would hike down an all-terrain vehicle trail. I had no special feeling or idea what to expect, but figured it was just as good a place to hunt as any. Before I left the truck, I noted the temperature gauge. It was 18 degrees. The sky was crystal clear, and the stars shown like millions of tiny, brilliant diamonds. The ground was noisy and crunched with every footstep. It was a quarter moon, and at six thirty, the sky on the eastern horizon spoke whispers of just hints of the coming light. It was crisp.

I felt comfortable as I layered up with thermals, my wool sweater, a fleece stocking cap, wool gloves, and my Game Hide jacket. It's not actual game hide, that's just the brand. I also wore my Norwegian military issue, gray wool pants. They are the best cold weather hunting pants I have ever owned. I found them at an army surplus store in Washington State many years ago. This morning I knew I needed to get somewhere and hunker down until the morning light broke. The ground was too crunchy to keep walking.

Within 300 yards of walking on the ATV trail I could see a meadow opening on my left. I could not tell the overall size, but it looked large enough and I could make out features several hundred yards out. Your eyes tend to adjust in the dark. It's never as dark as one may think. As I moved down the trail, I spotted several trees on the up slope. This seemed like a good area to settle in and watch the morning sunrise. I spotted a large pinion pine with large drooping boughs. As I ducked beneath the tree, I pulled off my small pack with my butcher knife and a few day provisions. I sat down against the trunk of the tree and placed my rife next to me on the ground.

Over the years, I developed a particular pet peeve. I truly dislike sitting on cold or wet surfaces. Not when I can avoid it. Hence, as part of my necessary gear, I carry an inflatable insulated pad to sit on. It makes the experience much more enjoyable, at least for me. With my cold weather clothing, a small thermos of hot coffee, and warm buns I was comfortable even at 18 degrees.

When hunting, I have learned being able to hear is a necessary skill. It also brings a gentle peacefulness to the surrounding. It is a meditative state of mind when I am in the wilderness listening. This is a most enjoyable time. I have seen so many glorious silent sunrises. Watching the forest wake up is a religious experience. It is the smallest of creature that tends to stir first. The finches, the field mice, the chipmunks. Then the larger critters, the jays, bobwhites, grouse, and coyotes. One can hear the coyotes start to yip and howl just before sunrise. The cries echo, almost ghost like, through the trees and off the hills. It is a magical time of the morning. It is the witching hour. It's the chipmunks that speak the loudest as they scurry from tree to tree looking for that morning breakfast of pine nuts. They chatter constantly, announcing to other creatures "Beware, you're on my turf." Then woodpecker's pick-up the pace, hiding in the high stands of pines, chipping away for the morning buffet of insect morsels.

It was just after the sunlight was needling through the trees, I heard a cow elk chirp. It came from somewhere behind me. I thought. "This could get interesting." I thought. Within a few minutes I heard several branches breaking. Looking to my right, about 40 yards off, a cow elk appeared. Then another and another. They moved quietly and gracefully into the meadow. I watched as they slowly moved across my field of vision for about two minutes. They vanished into the forest below my position. I have been on many hunts when I did not see any game. This was a treat to see elk on opening morning and not be detected.

We were on a spike hunt. This meant one can only harvest an elk with two single antlers. Thus, they are called spikes. Spikes are usually two years old and mostly fully grown. The Oregon Department of Fish and Wildlife has game management programs which target specific types of hunts to control game populations. Spike hunts are difficult as the animals are not as plentiful.

Seeing the elk caused my heart to race, and the adrenalin was flowing. I was no longer aware of the cold. As daylight broke, I looked from my position and noted I was sitting on the edge of a south facing saddle. This is a common topographical feature between two hills. A saddle is usually a well-traveled pathway for animals to get from one area to another. They are quick escape routes when being pursued. Seldom, if ever will an elk go over the top of a mountain. First off, it's too much work to go over the top. Second, crossing through a saddle reduces the chance of being spotted. The cows I watched earlier were not in a big hurry.

Twenty minutes later, I heard crashing and breaking of branches off to my right again. I started to think an ATV was coming up from behind. The crashing became louder and more intense. I was sure I would be sharing my secret position with some person on an ATV. Then everything went silent. After about a minute, I heard the crunch of the frozen ground. I spotted the nose of an elk popping out from behind a tree. It took a step out of the cover. It was another cow, then another and another. Then a branch antlered bull, then more cows. Thirteen in total, lined up like the Rockettes, high-stepping forty yards from me. They moved across my field of vison for the next few minutes, in no hurry. They had no idea I was watching. No spikes in the bunch. The small herd grazed into the forest below. I heard crunching off to my right again, and my heart was racing. Another cow and another and another and another. They meandered across the meadow following the trail, nipping at early morning forage along the way. No spikes.

I started to realize this was a well-used saddle and it was nothing but pure luck I landed here. As I sat, I heard the ravens call to each other announcing the race was on to find food for the morning. I could hear the pounding of their wings against the air, rhythmic whooshes of the black feathered trickster. In Northwest Native American mythology, Raven is the powerful figure who transforms the world. Stories and legends tell how Raven created the land, released the people from a cockle shell, and brought them fire. Raven stole the light and brought it out to light up the world. Raven is known as the trickster and can bring both good omens and bad. I figured brother Raven brought me good fortune so far.

I was brought out of this musing by more rhythmic crunching. Looking to my right, another cow elk appeared, and another, and another and another and another. They were like a chorus line. No spikes. I thought about the statistical probability of this happening. I thought about my friend Gerald. He could figure this out. He's a biostatistician. What is the ratio of spike elk to cow elk in this game management unit? How many more elk do I need to see in order to find a spike? I was lucky to see any elk, let alone twenty-four on opening morning. What are the chances?

Off to my right, I heard more crunching. Another cow was moving along to catchup with the rest. I silently watched her move off into the forest below. Shortly after that, 6 black-tail deer moved across the meadow, grazing silently, ears moving to catch any whisper of danger. Then a coyote, hunting field mice, silently crossed from my left to my right. I watched him as he stared at the ground and then pounced for a mouse.

As the sun moved higher, I started to feel the warmth. I stayed in my secret spot for eight hours. About 2:30pm 2NN called on the radio to check in. We talked briefly and decided to meet back at the truck. He had seen a lone cow moving over a ridge. We would see numerous more elk during our week of hunting. More bulls and more cows, but no spikes. Hunting spikes is difficult. We would not harvest an animal this year. But that's okay. There is so much more to hunting. It is a primal experience. It's facing the elements and being as prepared as you can be and accepting the gifts the great creator provides. This year, I did not experience the convergence I desired in the woods. Maybe next year I'll have better luck.

# Elk Hunt 2021

Log Entry#1
November 6, 2021—Ukiah Oregon—Basecamp
Stagecoach Stop

It was in the mid-20's this morning. There was a thin coat of ice on the truck. The ground was crunchy. I was hunting with 2NN again. He is a good hunting partner. He is part Hoopa Indian from Northern California. Stealthy and brave kind of guy. He is five years older than I. His bones are also aching. Aching bones are common trait for boomers. I did not hear a lot of shooting this morning. Maybe one or two distant shot a few miles south. We did not see any elk over the last day while scouting. We did find several areas with plenty of sign. My style of hunting has changed over the years. I find sitting and glassing large areas usually pays off. I have learned to let the younger hunters push the elk around. When I was younger, I use to think I could catch up to an elk wandering through the forest. I had the stamina to walk miles up and down mountains chasing the yellow ass of elk and pushing them into other hunters. Last year we were into several hundred elk, just no spikes. Spike hunts are tough.

Over the years I have learned how smart and crafty elk can be. They have a sixth sense of awareness. We used to have that awareness also, but evolution didn't think we would need it and it has faded away. Elk have been pursued by predators for eons. Seriously, for a few ten million years, elk have been the desired diet for cougars, bears, wolves, and humans. Their job is to escape at all costs and live to reproduce, and they do. Personally, I think the meat is the healthiest on the planet. It's pure, no steroids or vaccinations. No corn lot feeding bins or special diets other than the rich organic greens in the forest. A full-grown Rocky Mountain elk can easily sustain a family of four for a year. So can a Roosevelt elk, but for a bit longer because they are larger animals. Roosevelts are typically found in the coastal range west of the Cascade Mountains. I have hunted and harvested both. I often get into discussions as to why I hunt. I started hunting in earnest about thirty-five years ago. But before that I was introduced into the primal ritual in nineteen sixty-four when I was six years old.

I recall the first time I was witness to a deer taken by a true hunter. That hunter was a man I fondly refer to as "Uncle Richard" although we were not related by blood. My Uncle Richard and Aunt Arce and family of three boys and one daughter lived in Del Rio, Texas. We knew them through a relationship my mother developed with Aunt Arce while in business school and strengthened by other connections in Del Rio. My dad and Uncle Richard leased some land in the far desert of West Texas near the town of Pumpville fall of 1964. Pumpville is a tiny town with a population of twenty-six. It was a watering stop for steam trains while on cross country runs. Our deer camp consisted of my dad, my brother and I, our cousin Michael, Uncle Richard and his three boys Micky, Jimmy, and Tommy. They invited one of their friends to come along also. We arrived late in the afternoon and set up tents, a place to cook and wash, stacked limestone rocks for a fire ring, gather firewood, and dug a latrine. That was my job. There was a campfire that night and remember lots of laughing and stories until late. The next morning, my dad woke us up before daylight. Everyone was accounted for except Uncle Richard. He was already gone. I did not think much about it at that age but getting an early start to hunt is important. My dad walked us out in the morning chill as the sun was beginning to crest over the horizon. The west Texas sky was on fire with high clouds of bright reds and yellows. My brother and I had Ruger semi-automatic twenty-two rifles with scopes dad bought at Sears (remember Sears?). It was all he could afford at the time and probably a good choice given our limited knowledge of guns, hunting and life in general. I did not think about it then, but you really cannot bring a Whitetail deer down with a twenty-two unless you were Anne Oakley, or Patrick MacManus. All I recall is that I had a loaded gun for the first time in my life. It was a big deal to a six-year-old.

My dad positioned us along the dirt road we drove in on the previous afternoon. He told us not to move, keep quiet, and keep our eyes and ears open. He said a deer could come by at any time. I remember it was cold and I was shivering. One of the laces on my black canvas Keds tennis shoes snapped when I put them on in the dark tent. I was sitting alone on a flat rock, within sight of my brother about one hundred yards off on one side and Jimmy one hundred yards off on the other side. I fumbled with my shoelace trying to tie it together with another square knot. There were so many knots on my shoes, they looked like a Chinese knot puzzle with frayed ends. To make the knot I whispered the square knot chant, "right over left, and under, left over right". Then I heard a crisp crack of a rifle far off in the distance. I turned in the direction it came and froze. I listened to the lingering report echoing off the steep limestone canyon walls. I didn't move for a long time. It was a sound I would never forget. I sat there motionless; my shivering stopped. A little while later my brother walked up and said it was time to go back to camp. When we returned my dad was sitting by the fire. We sat together for a good while in silence. The mesquite wood fire smelled good, and it was warm.

The other boys slowly came filtering back. The chatter and buzz were exciting. Who got a shot off was the question? It was Uncle Richard. After about an hour or so, we spotted him carrying a deer draped across his shoulder. As we ran out to meet him, there were lots of yips and yells of success. He gently placed the carcass of a whitetail four-point buck deer down on the ground. He asked us to carry it by the antlers and legs the last one hundred yards to camp. The deer was heavy, and I had difficulty gripping its leg. Once back at camp I watched Uncle Richard take care of the animal. He spoke to me softly as he worked, peeling back more of the hide with his sharp knife, explaining what he was doing. The other boys were wandering off in different directions to hunt. He told me it was important to get the meat cooled down as quickly as possible. He propped the chest cavity open with a stick. The entrails were gone, left at the kill site somewhere in the next draw. "The coyotes will eat them." He spoke. Uncle Richard showed me where the scent stacks were located, about mid-hind-leg. He said he always cut the sacks out, or the musky scent would flow back into the meat. Some people like venison with that flavor and some didn't. He didn't particularly care for it that way. I sat for a long time looking at the dead animal after he left. I poked around, felt the smooth but hard earthy brown antlers, stroked the smooth gray and white hide looking for the bullet hole, and closely examined the coal black split hooves, and touched his large dark and blankly staring eye. It was at that moment I felt an electric connection that seared in me a desire to hunt. It was a primal instinctual drive. It was my first awareness of death. It was a connection to part of the collective DNA that binds us to everything past, present, and future. It was an enigmatic and distant feeling that haunts me to this day.

The plan was to go back on top of a plateau where 2NN hunted last year and drop him off. He would hunt from the top. I would go to the bottom of the large draw near Jenkins Corner. I killed an elk near Jenkins Corner two years earlier. We would meet in the middle. 2NN had a feeling. He always has a feeling. The elk were already being pushed around after several earlier hunts. I thought the best bet was to sit for a while and glass a large open park and watch. This strategy worked for me in the past. It takes a lot of patience. The forest is peaceful except for the occasional ATV that run a spaghetti network of designated trails. You can hear them coming a long way off. I know the elk avoid them and they hear a thousand times better than a human. They can smell you a mile away, and you can smell them but not quite a mile away. They have a musky and earthy odor. Once you get a good whiff, you will never forget it. I like the smell. It's wild and unique.

It's good to get the whiff because you know they are close, and they probably have not smelled you. The bulls have the strongest aroma.

We were up early and out the door by 5:15am. It was 26 degrees at on top of the grade near a gravel pit. That's where I left 2NN. The gravel pit is great landmark, even in the dark. The stars were exceptionally brilliant. They always are because the air is so clear and there are so few lights. There were a few shadowy clouds high in the northern sky. Elk had been in this area in the recent past. During the morning we didn't see anything that excited us about the area, so we kept looking farther afield. The elk sign we were seeing was about week old. You can tell because of the color, moister content, smell, and taste. It was a peaceful day in the forest. The tall pine trees swayed gently in the winds. I watched two whitetail deer feed just above me. I watched them for about three minutes. They had no idea I was there. We did not see any elk the entire day.

Log Entry #2
November 7, 2021—Base camp Stagecoach Stop-
Ukiah Oregon

We planned to cross Bridge Creek and hunt in one of the large canyons just below the wildlife refuge plateau. He commented that finding a spike is like looking for a needle in a haystack. The problem was getting across the creek. It's not a babbling brook kind of creek. It is wide and deep in many places and the vegetation around it is thick. It's not an easy crossing. There are no bridges, which I found ironic for a location with bridge in its name. It's a good area to hunt because many are not willing to cross the creek and travel up the steep canyons. To complicate the crossing, there are river rocks of all sizes, and they are unstable. It is an easy place to twist your ankle. The various sized stones, rocks, cobbles, and boulders would be good material for building a house. As we were making our plan, I suggested we find a ten-to-twelve-foot plank to place at likely crossing. I had seen such boards in discard piles in the town of Ukiah. 2NN suggested we find a log or such to make the bridge. I spotted a likely candidate and we pulled apart a tall rotting tree stump. We were able to salvage a ten-foot section. It was stable enough and we carried it to the truck. When we arrived at the creek to construct our makeshift bridge, someone else was parked in our spot. 2NN noticed a hunter walking out. We watched him closely. He crossed the creek in the vicinity we were considering to cross. He did get wet. We talked with him for a short while. He had a buddy coming down the canyon a bit behind him. He told us they had seen a few elk but nothing to shoot earlier in the day. He commented that finding a spike is like looking for a needle in a haystack. The canyons were big steep haystacks.

After talking with 2NN, we decided to deploy the bridge anyways. Getting the plank down the embankment was slow. Once I reached the bank, I was trying to position myself, and the plank, and balancing on lose rocks. I slipped into the creek up to my waist. It was exactly what I was trying to avoid doing. My boots and wool pants got soaked and the water was cold. I hate having wet boots. They take a long time to dry out. Wet wool is no picnic either. We kind of abandoned that plan, but we did have it as a backup. It was not all bad. I was able to place the plank in a sturdy place, wedged it some of the rocks. We could access the area later if we chose. Based on the information the other hunter provided, we were not in any hurry to ford the creek and scramble up the steep ravines.

From there we headed up in elevation to the Bridge Creek Wildlife Refuge, above the creek, to glass some large open parks. We were not alone. As evening approached, we were joined by ten other trucks with scores of hunters inside. They were looking with spotting scopes and binoculars just as we were. We only spotted a small deer herd of twelve. The others may have spotted something, but I didn't think so. We cut out for the cabin just as the sun was setting. I was ready to get out of my wet boots. The sky was red and yellow with deep gray pillows of clouds building in the east. When we arrived at basecamp, another hunter was coming in. He had blood on his hands. He was excited and told us he got into a huge herd of one thousand elk. There were numerous spikes. He said he had trouble picking one out because there were so many critters running all over the place. He gave us the general location and went on to explain the elk were scattered all over near the highway because a pack of wolves chased them from their normal hangouts. He kept saying the main herd was over one thousand strong. It sounded too good to be true. If it sounds too good to be true, it's not true.

2NN and I talked about his story. The fact of the matter was, he had an elk, and we didn't. We had not seen any fresh sign either. We figured it was just as good a place to hunt as any other at this point. When the hunter described his kill and road numbers associated with the approximate location; his story changed. Another thing he said that bothered me was he just opened the door to his truck and shot. If he was on a highway, I had my doubts it was a legal harvest. 2NN heard it also and was confused with what he was saying. Now something I have learned over the years; you don't give away your secret hunting location. Ever. You send the newbies as far away from your secret hunting location as you can. If you can convince them to hunt in the next county, do it. We had our reservations, but we didn't have anything to lose by driving up into the area. Elk can appear out of nowhere. We had a plan. That evening we had 2NN's venison stew. It was delicious.

Log Entry #3
November 8, 2021- Base camp Stagecoach Stop—
Ukiah Oregon

Out the door by 5:30am. We headed up highway fifty-one and turned off just before Texas Bar. 2NN has a GSP chip with most of the back roads identified. So, we had a pretty good idea of where we were going. What we did not count on was the number of hunting camps. Not just in this area, but all over the Ukiah unit. There are trailers of all sized, age, and shape and there are wall tents of all sizes, shapes, and materials. We drove to the end of a gravel road. It was still dark. The ground was noisy, it was frozen. The surface was networked with elongated ice crystals that sounded like popcorn going off with each step. So much for being quite I thought. Walking in the dark of morning is peaceful. Your eyes adjust. You can make out the trees and opening, shadows and lighter areas. Evolution has provided humans with unique capabilities for vision, hearing, smelling, tasting and travel when in the dark. I moved about five hundred yards from the truck and found a place on the edge of a clearing to sit and wait. I have carried an insulated pad to sit on for years. I hate having cold or wet buns. It's the small creature comforts that make the experience that much more enjoyable. Good gloves, a warm wool hat, insulated layered clothing, and warm socks are necessary articles.

While sitting quietly, my mind wanders to all types of brain regions, especially fun memories. I remember friends I have hunted with over the years. Other than Uncle Richard, another individual that influenced my hunting was Chuck Hellier. I'll never forget Chuck. I met him through a friend while I was working at the Hanford Nuclear Reservation. He was vice president of Eberline Services, a company that provided health physics support to projects across the site. Chuck, in my opinion, was a man's man. He was six foot five, from Norwegian heritage. He was a retired U.S. Army Colonel, with numerous decorations from his military career including two Purple Hearts. He was probably one of the kindest and most generous individuals I have ever known. His family was from Pennsylvania and that is where he learned to hunt. He was a great hunter. He had the awareness of animals. Chuck was particular in some unique ways. He enjoyed his afternoon cocktail and eating lots of good food. He was a master chef. Chuck was stationed in Europe a few times over his career. He was a Jägermeister, a hunting master in Germany. He told the story of taking a Red Deer Stag. He took the required one hundred question hunting exam, and the royal Jägermeister organization was impressed with his perfect score. He was given permission to hunt in a prestigious reserve in the Black Forest, reserved for nobility. He was instructed what to shoot. He was ready. When a stag appeared about four hundred yards out, he shot it. It was a beautiful mature male stag. What Chuck did not know about but learned quickly, were the unwritten traditions and customs that went along with the sport. I recall Chuck saying that stag cost him several extra thousand marks in dinner and drinks after the hunt. Whoever shoots the stag was obligated to treat the entire hunting party. I think he said his hunting party was comprised twelve others and the festivities were held in an ancient hunting lodge. His stag is hanging in that hall along with many others as tradition dictated. He said the only thing he received was a rather large bill. But he would not change a thing. He remains friends with that hunting group and he is welcome to come on a hunt anytime.

2NN and I did not see any elk in the location described the night before. We did see lots of Whitetail. I could tell there were some healthy herds in this area. The sun was out again, and I took a nice nap around noon. I think the elk were also napping about that time. It was a pleasant day. We covered a good amount of ground but saw no elk.


Log Entry #4
Tuesday November 9, 2021- Ukiah Oregon


In a lifetime, opportunities will occasionally materialize. I have always wanted to own real estate. I noticed a realtor sign while we were driving from one area to another. I took a picture of it. I googled for the listing and found a piece of property that looked interesting. It was private land surrounded by National Forest and Bureau of Land Management property. Another interesting point was the cabin. It was listed as a dry cabin. It was in the Ukiah hunting unit. There would always be elk.

I told 2NN I wanted to see the land and decided to head that way in the morning. We would hunt along the way. We needed to travel through several miles of private land but there was a right of way providing access. Within three quarters of a mile of reaching public lands, I spotted three elk off to my right. It was still first light. 2NN stopped the truck and I got my rifle, and chambered a round. I keep four rounds hot. One in the chamber and three in the clip. We knew that elk would wait for a vehicle to pass by before they calm down. I told 2NN to drive on and I would stalk the elk and see if there were more. As he drove on, I watched the elk. I saw the three but no more. I was able to get within two hundred yards of them. It was a combination of the elk moving in my direction and me slowly moving to trees for cover. There was a bench feature just below the road. The elk were out of sight and on a flat feeding spot. It was a beautiful set up. I could see several hundred yards around me, and there were Pondarosa Pines scattered about. It would have been an easy shot if a spike appeared. The three eventually drifted back into the forest. I was pretty sure they were just a small group. 2NN drove down about a half a mile and parked. I backed out and head up to the road, it was drizzling lightly, and the air smelled clean and fresh.

2NN got turned around in the forest later that morning. It's easy to do. While he was spinning around getting unlost, I hiked to the property. I took the liberty of trespassing and toured the cabin and the immediate surrounding and structures. The cabin had been vacant for years. It was dry, but the forest critters had taken over years ago. It could be rebuilt. There is a rule that provides for structures in-place before the rules were promulgated, it's called bring grandfathered in. A grandfather clause for certain classes of property. I believed this one fit the clause. I would have to verify this with the county. I had come across this on another property I was interested in in the coastal range. I missed out on that one. These types of properties don't come up for sale very often.

I hunted a few more roads and then turned my compass to service road 025 about 2 miles away. The area I was in was much too tight to hunt. The vegetation was thick and the likelihood of seeing an elk and getting a shot off were slim. It started to sleet and then snow. The world quiets down when it snows. A stillness surrounds you. You hear nothing. It was a peaceful walk back. We made it back to the truck and headed to an area for an evening hunt. We went to an area off the 0240 road. It was snowing lightly.

The forest was quiet, and it looked elky. About four in the afternoon, I heard wolves in the distance. One first then several others joined in. It was eerie and beautiful. We heard two evenings before that a pack of wolves was chasing one of the larger elk herds. The herd was several hundred strong. The wolves would break-up the herd into smaller groups or pods. The three I ran into earlier was a small pod. No spikes in that pod. The cry of the wolves was a cry to gather the others in the area for a hunt in the evening I thought. Or they may be coming for me. Although I have never had to use it, I carry a nine millimeters pistol with me. It's added weight, but you never know. A few minutes later I heard another pack of wolves off to my right, due south of where I was standing. Then I heard another pack from east of my position. I figured all three packs were not more than three to five hundred yards out from me. From where I was, I had a good field of fire. I could see something coming two hundred yards out. The sun was setting, and it had quit snowing. Light was beginning to fade, and the wolves had gone into silent mode. They were meeting to setup an elk hunt, although I would not be a contest for a pack of hungry wolves. Shooting time ends thirty minutes after sunset and my light was fading fast. I did not relish a confrontation with any wolves, so I quietly backed to and hiked the half mile back to the truck. 2NN was waiting. It was a good day in the woods.

Log Entry #5
Wednesday November 10, 2021—Ukiah Oregon

Slow day in the forest. Saw a few whitetail deer. No elk. Walked a lot up several draws. Did not see a lot of tracks even with the half inch of snow on the ground. Covered a lot of ground.

Log Entry #6
Thursday November 11, 2021 (Veterans Day) Ukiah Oregon

It rained throughout the day. Not a hard pounding rain. Not the rain that hits asphalt and concrete. It was calming as it hit the forest floor, dripping off the tall Ponderosa pine and Juniper trees. It is soft to the ears. It's a gentle, peaceful and easy feeling that lightly dances on the forest bed of light brown pine needles. The ground is silent as you walk through the forest. I listen and watch carefully. I'm looking and listening for the odd movement or sound. The one that may be a large snapping branch or a high-pitched cry of the hawk, or the chatter of a pesky squirrel. I found a place which afforded me a great view of a saddle crossing. It is used by lots of game and trails are networked through the area like a great bowl of discarded shoestrings. This area gets used a lot. I sat there and waited.

The silence gives me time. Personal time is so precious. Time spent with oneself is time well spent. My success rate for hunting elk is not good. I have been hunting for thirty-five years. I have personally harvested only four elk. My sons have also harvested elk. I have taken deer and caught fish. It' good to eat what you harvest with your own hands. It tastes better and there is a certain amount of appreciation for the skills involved. It's a primal feeling of completeness. But not for everyone.

Log Entry #7
Friday November 12, 2021, Outside Ukiah Oregon

Off road 54 to the east. Day 7-the last day of the hunt. It's been a long week. we've seen all types of weather. From eighteen degree to fifty-four. Snow, drizzle, and sunshine. The forest looks and smells healthy. I spotted five elk this year. Four cows and one calf. They were all healthy and beautiful. No spikes. This hunt is one of the most difficult to hunt. If you play by the rules, statistically only sixteen percent of the hunters in Ukiah unit harvest a spike. Slim odds but what a chase. It's a fair chase. My bones are feeling my age. My left hip is starting to give me trouble after a week of working it out. We did not harvest an elk this year. But we tried. So, what is it about elk hunting that keeps me coming back? It must be the feeling of challenging oneself to do something. It's the feeling of the contest of animal verses man. If one cannot find invigoration in the challenge, then what else is there? The people along the way add a spice to the challenge.

I am hopeful 2NN and I will be able to hunt together next year. We keep talking about having our sons hunt with us. We need that to happen. I toasted Uncle Richard and Chuck Hellier this evening with one shot of Jägermeister. They bring back good memories.

# The Extraordinary Young Scout

**W**HEN I FIRST MET COLIN, I DID NOT KNOW WHAT TO think. He obviously had severe disabilities. His older brother had joined our scout troop and I told his mom that Colin was welcome to join if she thought it would be a safe environment for him. With some trepidation, she told me that he falls down a lot and that he needed to avoid hitting his head. She said he had a malformed brain. I did not know quite how to respond other than I would do my best to watch over him if he joined the troop. Over the course of the next month, I was able to have several brief conversations with Colin. He seemed like a good kid, but not typical in any sense of the word. He was extraordinary. He always seemed to smile.

Colin is about 4'8" with a thick mop of curly brown hair. He can walk, but it is difficult. His motor skills are impacted due to his brain not being fully developed. He walks with what I would describe as "crazy legs." His gait is uneven; his legs do not move in a smooth pattern, but rather with a jolting strain and with an uneasy but determined effort. He tries to run, but it is difficult as his body shifts erratically to try to balance. He would occasionally lose his balance and fall. His arms are much the same, moving in what appears to be erratic flailing patterns. He wears glasses with thick "coke bottle" lenses. You can see that he has had numerous surgeries on his hands and fingers that allow him to grasp simple objects like pencils and paper. Despite all of this, Colin was always smiling.

As the troop was preparing to head to summer camp, I asked his mom if he would be going. At first, she did not think it would be a very good idea. She brought up the issue of Colin falling and hitting his head. If he did, it could cause additional issues and a trip to the emergency room (or worse, I imagined). She told me that Colin needed constant care; he needed help dressing and using the restroom. I could tell in her voice that it would be a risk and a lot of additional effort. Again, I told her that I would be as supportive as I could, and I was sure some of the other scouts would help as needed. After a little persuasion, she agreed to the idea, stating that the only way it would work was if she came to camp as well. I totally agreed as I needed a 2nd adult anyway.

Over the next few weeks, as we began final preparations for camp, I could sense Colin was getting excited about the adventure. His mom asked many questions about the camp and what to expect. We would be sleeping on platform tents. The tents are canvas, placed over a simple A-frame structure on a wooden deck. Most scouts bring a pad for comfort and a sleeping bag. One thing that was not expected was the number of daddy-long-legs spiders roosting in the eves of the tents. The scouts found this to be a bit unsettling, except Colin. He did not seem to mind sharing the tent with the long-legged arachnids. We would have meals in the dining hall with about 300 other hungry, adolescent kids from Oregon, Washington, and California. Although the dining room seemed chaotic during mealtimes, a certain structure and flow was evident. The staff had done this many times before and honed the feeding of scouts down to a fine art.

As the week at camp continued, I was able to spend a fair bit of time with Colin. I kept going over the Scout Law with him with the hope he would be able to remember it and work towards getting his Scout rank. Scout is the first rank for all the boys (and girls) entering the program. After a while, and numerous attempts, I would start the law saying, "Colin, a scout is…" waiting for him to respond. Colin would respond with "Helpful". I would tell him, yes as scout is helpful but that's not the first point of the law; it's "Trustworthy." Colin would repeat that a scout is Trustworthy and then he would say that a scout is "nice", and I would tell him that yes a scout is nice, but the term we use is "Kind" and that was the sixth point. After that, I would recite the entire law and Colin would repeat the words after me. Then we would start again. I would ask Colin to help me recite the Law, "A scout is..." and Colin would say "Helpful." This pattern would be repeated throughout the week. As far as Colin was concerned, above all, a Scout is helpful and nice.

Colin would make it to numerous activities located all over the camp. The camp is located on over 400 acres owned by the Boy Scouts of America. Activities included every-thing from rifle shooting, archery, swimming, climbing, nature studies, pioneering, and of course, eating. He tended to spend a lot of time working hard on his Scout rank with his mom. He practiced tying a square knot, a clove hitch, a bowline, a taut line and practiced identifying plants and ani-mal signs. I spent time checking up on my other scouts, and tending to administrative issues with merit badge classes, scouts with complaints about food, unfair course leaders, how far apart activities were, bee stings and how bored some were. Not Colin. He was smiling. When I would meet up with him, I would start the Scout Law..." Colin, a Scout is?" and his response was always helpful and nice. I could tell he was having a blast. His mom was also smiling.

During the second day, the camp holds a Polar Bear Plunge. The event takes place at 6:30AM at the waterfront. Colin decided that he wanted to do the plunge, and he did. He is not a swimmer by any stretch, but mom brought his life vest and Colin was the first to jump in with a huge smile. He had no fear. This set the pace for Colin's activities during the week. The camp offered two Polar Bear Plunges and Colin did them both and motivated most of the troop to do the second plunge with him. Colin received a special patch from the waterfront director for this. Colin decided he was going to climb the 40ft-climbing tower and after being secured in a harness, he did. He made the climb, not once but three times. Colin decided he wanted to try archery and on his own he was able to hit not only the target, but also the bulls-eye numerous times. He got a little help from the archery program director. Colin decided he wanted to try shooting a .22 rife, and with a little help he did. He asked if he could try shooting the 10-gauge shotgun and with a little help from mom he did, saying after the first shot, "Wow, that was cool, but it sure kicked my shoulder." Colin decided he wanted to work on some merit badges, and he was able to complete the Art and Nature Study badges. His determination was amazing. None of this was easy for Colin, but he met every challenge with a smile.

As the week progressed, the troop helped in so many ways to include Colin in all the activities he could manage.

A scout would take his hand and walk slowly with him up the trail or they would help his mom by pushing Colin in his special "Bob" three-wheeled buggy to meals or to opening and closing flag ceremonies and to the campfire programs. The Troop rallied around Colin because Colin was inspiring the scouts. The scouts would help Colin with meals and getting him ready to go to certain activities. The scouts helped get Colin to the top of a 60ft. sand dune and back down.

What we did not realize at the time was that Colin was really helping us. Colin was displaying a scouting spirit and courage that was truly inspirational. It was infectious, contagious to all. To see this young man, with such apparent disabilities, striving to do the best he could and engage in as much of life as he could, made others aware of their abilities. Colin added a dimension of diversity to the troop and the troop responded by being inclusive and caring and thinking not of themselves, but others. I think they have learned something far greater than any merit badge would teach and that is the power of being helpful and nice.

As we were preparing for camp, one of the goals the troop established was to try to achieve the coveted recognition of Honor Troop. The Camp Director and staff give this award to a troop that can complete numerous tasks. Items include service projects, rank advancement, merit badge completions by all troop members, participation in camp wide games and other requirements. The

Scoutmaster must also complete several tasks to support the award. One of which includes 2 tours of duty in the "Dish Pit". The dish pit is where (as the name infers) the dish washing happens. It is an industrial dish washing operation with a large stainless steel high temperature dish washing machine and rinse off area where 300 plus trays are cleaned and sanitized for the next meal. The task also includes washing pots, pans, glasses, and silverware. During one of the lunch periods, I was sitting with Colin, and I told him I had to go do my task of washing dishes for camp. Colin immediately asked if he could help me. I told him that it was a task for the Scoutmaster; I thanked him and headed to the kitchen. After a few minutes in the pit, I thought Colin might find it interesting to see what this industrial operation looked like with the loud noises of the kitchen, water going everywhere, people yelling orders and the mountain of dirty dishes to be cleaned. I asked one of the assistant cooks to go get Colin just so he could see the operation. By this time everyone in camp knew Colin and the cook agreed. As Colin was escorted in, I turned to him and smiled; he smiled back. He moved close to me and asked, "Can I help you?"

I told him again, that this was a job for the Scoutmaster so that we could try to get Honor Troop. What I did not tell him was that he had already helped me. He helped me see and appreciate what true scout spirit looks like. Colin has helped me see the many blessings I have, and he has helped me appreciate what it is to be helpful and nice.

I don't think Colin will ever get to the rank of Eagle Scout as outlined in the requirements by the Boy Scouts of America. In my book he already is an Eagle Scout. Yes, Colin, a Scout is helpful, and a Scout is nice. Thank you for being so very helpful, so very nice and so extraordinary. Thank you for inspiring me to use my abilities to be the most helpful and nice person that I can be.

# Angel

I AM NOT SURE HOW GOD GIVES OUT BRAINS, BUT WHEN thinking back about my cousin Angel he got a strange one. His brain probably resembled an old coal fire train engine that smoked a lot and didn't get much maintenance as opposed to the modern and efficient electro-magnetic high-speed trains around nowadays most normal folks have. But at the time I thought Angel was one of the smartest people I knew or ever expected to know. There wasn't anything he didn't know or couldn't figure out. He was only a few years older than me, and I followed him around like a pup as he espoused knowledge and wisdom. It was not only amazing, but downright scary how much he knew about every subject under and over the sun. That was before his brain started to give out, about the time I entered high school. That's when I started to detect certain inconsistencies in the information I was getting. When I pointed out some of the errors in his information, he claimed his head was too full and sometimes mixed things up. He told me that's what happens when people get too smart.

As the years went by, Angel's intellect continued to spiral downwards. He eventually leveled out to what he termed a bit above average, but to me resembled the intelligence of a Thresher woodpecker. But before that, during my formative years, he would tell me everything about everything. He knew everything about cars, guns, sex, outer space, life, females, death, hunting, aliens, engines, fishing, wildlife, girls, movies, music, sex, motorcycles, fashion, haircuts, and hamburgers. He enjoyed being outdoors and dreamed about living off the land like a mountain man.

Once, when we were walking through the woods, I spotted a squirrel with a big furry gray tail going up a tree and asked Angel what kind of squirrel it was. "A special tree squirrel." He said, "You know. That squirrel climbs trees for a living. That's why he's named a tree squirrel." He went on to explain, "That there is a special squirrel. He eats nuts and hides them in the ground." Angel knew unique things about all kinds of animals. I later learned just about every squirrel climbed trees and buries nuts in the ground.

He owned a hunting dog he named Sister, because she looked like his sister or rather his sister looked like the dog. I don't remember which. She didn't do too much that

I can recall. As a matter of fact, the only time I saw her move was when Angel called her to dinner. She moved like greased lighting when she needed to. Her manners were atrocious, and she consumed her rations like a starving rat. She then returned to her familiar bloated position, sleeping on the sofa, legs splayed in all directions, ignoring everything but the dinner yell. Nothing ever motivated Sister except food and the male Bassett hound that lived down the road about ten miles. Every now and then she disappeared for a few days, coming home looking a little rough-shod and worn-out, grinning from ear to ear, looking for food. Other than that, the old girl was home to a carnival of fleas and ticks that found her a stationary tropical hairy island paradise. I think she like the attention. To be truthful, I don't believe his dog ever hunted.

Angel always thought he was a smart when it came to money. He thought he knew how to make the best of deals. When he turned sixteen, he took me with him to buy his first car from a local car lot called "Lucky's Cars". He was eyeballing a 1965 Toyota corolla that resembled a car. It had a steering wheel, four slick tires, all different sizes, an engine compartment with a running engine, no doors, and as the salesman Mr. Lucifer explained, it was easier to get out of when you came across wild game. Angel whispered to me, "Just like the real safari hunters in Africa". There was no glass in any of the windows. Mr. Lucifer explained it was a special safety feature; if a wild animal jumped in the way of the hunting rig, whoever was inside did not have to worry about getting covered with shattering glass. This feature was included at no extra charge. Angel was eating all this up. He really wanted this car but did not want to show his hand to Mr. Lucifer. Angel especially like the sunroof. It was welded or rather rusted in the open position so a hunter could be standing at the ready with his rifle, poking his head out of the top of the car if wild game came running by. "You could just pop your head out and shoot it." explained Mr. Lucifer.

The car had no front fenders either. This was a modification that kept the car from getting caught up in the brush. Another interesting feature Angel really like was the automatic smoke screen the car produced. The car billowed smoked between backfires, like a mobile Mt. Etna. It spewed a thick blue colored shield limiting visibility to about two feet. It was a magical smoldering smoke screen used to hide from wild game. The engine backfiring or warning gunshots was an additional feature that was hard to come by explained Mr. Lucifer. He told Angel he included all these enhancements at no additional cost. When Angel asked how much for rig, Mr. Lucifer declared he'd let it go for five hundred dollars and that was a deeply discounted, special, no-nonsense, fourth-of July, Memorial Day, winter end of the year inventory reduction doubly special price. Angle laughed cynically and started to walk away. Then, without any warning,

Angel turned around slowly, kicked the dirt a couple of times, not wanting to lose the deal offered him three hundred dollars and asked if that was enough to close the deal. Mr. Lucifer tripped and twisted his ankle as he ran to get the title and a sales receipt from his office. Lucifer handed Angel a receipt that said in big red letters, "NO RETURNS-AS-IS-NO-WARRENTY-EVER".

As we drove away, Angel was grinning ear to ear and could not believe how he was able to cheat Mr. Lucifer out of such a great hunting rig. He felt it was worth twice what he paid. He declared you could not find another rig like it in a hundred miles. It even had a squeaky back seat with a thick motheaten wool blanket included to cover the springs that had worn through the original vinyl. Angel explained if he ever had the chance, he could engage in nostalgic adolescence R-rated trysts, he whispered the backseat was perfect. On the way home Angel made use of the rusted holes in the floorboards. He said he was happy he was able to watch the road go by. It was "neat" and if he had to spit, he just huck a luggie between his feet. He was so proud of his first hunting rig. His dream of being a mountain man was coming true. He could now drive off into the hills and hunt all year round for food with Sister. Much to my surprise, Angel kept that car running all summer. Angel paid Mr. Lucifer to take the car back. Mr. Lucifer explained the car was a hazard to drive on the streets.

As Angel was growing up, he wandered through our small-town avoiding work, school and the local law enforcement officer named Deputy Honey. Honey was a diminutive young fellow who wore a large straw cowboy hat that wobbled on his shaved head. The hat also hid a nasty scar Honey said he got during an encounter with a mountain lion when he was a kid. The truth was his sister hit him on the head with a hammer for eating her pet rabbit. For some unknown reason Honey always had an eye out for Angel and wanted to talk with him about strange happening around town. Angel tried to avoid Honey because every time they talked, it turned into a sticky mess and ended up with a stern lecture on breaking the law and going to prison for life. One time, Angel found a perfectly good blue plastic comb in the street and put it in his pocket. That same afternoon Angel pulled it out to use it, Honey spotted him, stopped his police car, and yelled at him to "Halt, in the name of the law". Honey declared the comb was his and he unknowingly lost it earlier that day. Angel was arrested on a charge of petty theft. Angel, being the smart one, kept arguing what the heck Honey needed with a comb anyway? His head was as bald as a cue-ball! The town was hive of activity and buzzed with gossip for weeks. Angel ended up returning the comb, and all charges were dropped. That incident was the beginning of a lifelong battle of dull-witted woodpeckers. It was a continuous battle between good and evil. I never really figured out which one was good, and which one was evil.

Angel and I experienced many firsts together. One time, as his brains began to wither, he acquired a live horse. A live ten-dollar horse. The man Angel bought the animal from, Mr. Bill Trader, said the horse didn't look too good. But the horse looked good enough for Angel. What Trader should have said was the horse was part blind. He kept running into fences and doors open on his left side. Angel told me I could be part owner for free. All I needed to do to become an owner was help take care it at our family home. I instantly agreed not having any idea what I was getting into. Just the thought of owning part of a live horse was exciting to a nine-year-old. He told me I could ride Arlo, the horse, anytime he wasn't on board.

I should have asked which part I owned, because the next thing I knew I was monitoring the backend. Angel got the front end and said he would take care of feeding Arlo. He was indeed a shrewd businessman. The problem I learned, was Arlo was a constant flow of horse poop. I don't mean just a plop every now and then, I mean day in and day out the horse did not stop producing. It seemed like every few minutes, a twenty-foot mound of horse shit appeared. My job was to move the mounds from one place to another. We did not have a horse stall or corral, nor did we have a plan for the disposal of the waste. I ended up filling the family garbage can quickly, much to my parents' dismay, and every other bucket and bag I could find. The truly strange part of the ownership deal was I never saw Angel feed the beast. I didn't see the horse eat anything other than the grass and flowers and meager crops from our garden.

Being a horse owner, despite the part I owned, filled me with pride and pure joy until the first time I clamored on board the mighty steed. I was excited to ride off into the sunset like Rex Allen my cowboy hero, but Arlo refused to move. The horse wouldn't budge. After countless commands of "giddy-up" and gentle nudges from my tennis shoe covered feet, I declared the horse was broken and I didn't feel I was getting my horse owner needs met. Angel told me he would help and took a long flat board, wrapped the end with some rusted barbed-wire and whapped Arlo on the rump. Arlo reared up on two legs like Silver, the Lone Ranger's mighty stallion, and bolted. We didn't have a saddle, or bridle, or reins so I was left holding the hair on his neck has he raced down the dirt road at full speed losing my white canvass Keds tennis shoes in the first jolt of the ride. Ten miles down the road, where the Bassett hound lived, Arlo came to a slow walk looking anxiously over his rump for Angel. I was able to slide off the charge and started the grueling barefoot walk home. Sister, Angel's dog, appeared out of nowhere, grinning from ear to ear, and came along side of me. She looked rather tired as we walked at a slow pace for a long time, until she heard the dinner yell. She disappeared like a heat seeking missile leaving a dusty vapor trail in her wake. Arlo, our mighty stallion, was never seen again.

I'll never forget my cousin Angel. I learned a lot from him even though his train of a brain was missing some important parts. At some point Angel went into politics and ran for a seat in the US Senate. After months on the campaign trail, he lost the election but did get 10 votes. I wondered who voted for him.

# The Chickens

REMEMBER THE FIRST TIME I MET A CHICKEN FACE TO FACE. I was about four years old, on a visit to Grandma Diaz's house in Hondo, Texas. Hondo, in 1961, was much as it is today. Its population was 2,500 souls. The population of chickens was triple. Many of the coops backed up to railroad tracks running through the center of town. The area resembled a shanty town of rusted corrugated tin roofs and mis-matched weathered boards held together by a few nails and bailing wire. The railroad tracks ran smack-dab through the center of the town. A sign posted at the town limits read, "This is God's country. Please don't drive through it like hell!"

The message did not apply to trains. Two hundred car freight trains traveled through the town at what seemed like supersonic speeds, rattling houses, windows, rear molars, and every beer bottle in the pocket-sized metropolis. The chickens ran for shelter every time a train thundered through. A chicken unlucky enough to not get out of the way of a coming train, got sucked into the vacuum of death, and vanished. A puff of feathers usually lingered about. As a little kid, I often wondered what ever happened to those birds.

Grandma Diaz always kept a brood of hens. They free ranged all over the town, mingling with everyone else's chickens. There were chicken gangs that hung out in the dirt alleys and backstreets. The gangs included the Leghorns, the Brahmas, Orpingtons, Polish, Sussex and the badass Rhode Island Reds. Chicken fights were common. There was squawking, cackling, and crowing at all hours of the day and night, not to mention the swearing, cussing and the occasional shotgun blasts. It seemed like a shotgun blast was always followed by silence. Even the cussing and swearing stopped after a good blast or two.

The best fights involved the chickens from the other side of the tracks. The uppity chicks lived on that side. The Silkie's and Guineafowl were the most stuck-up. They were too good for the others. Every now and then a rumor would circulate about some chick being caught with one of the roosters from the wrong side of the tracks. Feathers would fly, accusations were made, and name cackling was squawked. About 21 days later, a hen would emerge from her coop sporting a shadow of shame, escorting a curious entourage of ten or twelve yellow puff balls. She and her brood wandered aimlessly around the town, being ostracized by all the other chicken gangs. No self-respecting chicken wanted to be associated with a hen of little virtue, much less her brood of squeaking little bastard chicks.

Grandma Diaz didn't care. She adopted more stray chicks than anyone else in town. It was a mixed lot of multi-colored birds that knew they had better lay eggs or the crazy woman with the axe was the last stop. I was the one asked to catch the slacking hens that stopped laying. The chickens were less afraid of me. Being a somewhat small kid, I was closer to the ground and enjoyed playing in the dirt. What self-respecting kid didn't play in the dirt at that young age? I even ate the bugs I found while scratching about. Heck, some of the worms were downright tasty. Nevertheless, Grandma Diaz always had fresh eggs.

I spent most of my time in Hondo playing with the chickens. I liked them. They all had individual personalities. I named almost all of them. There was One-eyed Pansy, Squeaky To-and-From, Bent-Wing Billie, Silly Sally, Voiceless Veronica, Fluffy Freida, Madam Curious, Jughead Judy, and many more. I was fascinated with the way they looked at me. They cocked their long necks and stared with their beady black eyes, deep into me as though they knew me. I was their protector or legal counsel or just a friend. I talked to them about everything, including my mean brother and sister. We squawked about the weather, they told me who was dating who, what chicken gangs to avoid and who the best-looking rooster was. It was general chicken gossip. I gave them the best advice a four-year-old could and they told me the truth about which came first, the chicken or the egg.

One of the roosters I named Bobby the Brainiac was smart. He belonged to an old German couple who lived a few houses from Grandma. Brainiac spoke German, English, Spanish and dog. Every morning when he crowed, his chicken voice had a discernable change in frequency. He started crowing early with one particular guttural tone. On cue, all the dogs in town began to howl together. That was followed by another distinct tone in his crowing and all the Mexicans would start yelling colorful words having to do with reproduction. Then Brainiac would begin to voice his early morning greeting in yet another tone and the farmers started to yell in English how good the rooster was for nothing. I thought that was a complement at the time. Finally, one more change in Brainiacs crowing stirred up the Germans. It was a cacophony of community unity. Everyone loved Brainiac. Until one morning, I recall hearing a shotgun blast about the time Brainiac was sending his good morning salute to the Mexicans. Then there was total silence. I think that's all I have to say about that.

Flash forward to 2020. Over the years, we have had several broods of chickens. There is something about fresh eggs but are they are worth it? Let's figure this out...

First, you need to have a space for the chickens to live. Preferably, not inside your house. I read that one healthy chicken needs a minimum of ten square yards to roam and call home. So, if you have ten chickens, you need one hundred square yards. That's about the size of Hondo, Texas. Next, you need a coop with nest boxes and chicken approved nesting material, whatever that is. Chickens are not that particular about where they lay eggs. It is not uncommon to find eggs in the most unusual places. For example, I have found eggs inside my car, on top of the roof and under the barbecue grill, in the dirt, and in a pond. Coops can cost nothing if you have a lot of junk laying around. On the other hand, one can have a coop resembling the Hurst Castle, with a moat, an automatic draw bridge, and hot and cold running water, heated nest boxes, and brick walls for a mere ten thousand dollars.

I imagine if the hens are from the other side of the tracks, the Hurst Castle Coop would fit right in. Then one needs to calculate the cost of chicken feed. Back in the old days, chickens ate what they could find. Grass, bugs, worms, nuts, dirt, other eggs. Everything organic. Now you can get all kinds of special feed. There is high test scratch, a combination of corn and seeds, and Monster Energy drinks to supplement the special steroid laced organic laying feed. There are numerous varieties laying feeds, some specially designed to improve egg laying efficiencies and make the shells bullet proof. The hens will never know what hit them as they are producing three eggs a day. A bag of feed can cost forty dollars for fifty pounds. A flock of ten hens can consume fifty pounds of feed in about three minutes. Seems the cost of an egg to feed ratio is not complicated. The solution is to go get eggs at the grocery store.

The coop will need maintenance and the mountains of chicken poop will need to be cleaned out regularly and disposed of. The poop can be used as a fertilizer, but I have learned it may be too rich in nitrogen and end up killing your garden. The fertilizer can be considered too hot and burn a hole in the ground clear to China. It is considered a hazardous material if you need to ship it offsite and will require a hazardous waste shipping manifest and special personal protective equipment and training for handling toxics. It will have to be triple bagged, and the shipping containers will have to be labeled and tagged with GPS sensors for tracking. They have an app for that. Currently there is an international ban on shipping chicken manure to other countries for disposal. Something about NAFTA, environmental justice and chicken manure legislation is being discussed in the highest echelons of Government.

At the time of this story, I have eighteen chickens. That was not the original plan. I discussed getting a few chickens with my family because I felt we would enjoy the fresh eggs. After researching places to pick-up chicks, I found a chicken ranch in Tangent, Oregon, not too far from home. I could have opted to get chicks shipped from a far-off state like Ohio, Nebraska, Wisconsin, or New York. I imagine it's traumatic for a chick to be put into a box and shipped via U.S. Postal Service. I don't think I would enjoy or survive the journey. One company stated that they did not warrant chicks, but always put a couple extra yellow puff balls in just in case one or two did not survive the journey. The chicken ranch in Tangent Oregon scheduled a hatch date and asked customers to come by at a certain time to collect pre-paid baby fowl. When I arrived, the chicken rancher said he threw in a couple of extra puff balls just in case one or two didn't make it home or there was a rooster or two among the clutch. Rooster? I had not considered getting a rooster. I ordered hens. The chicken rancher said he could not tell the sex of the young birds. To quell customer concerns, he threw in a couple of extra, just in case. I left with sixteen puffballs. I think he just wanted to get rid of the chicks.

About this same time, one of my sons asked if I would adopt two chicks from a friend. The friend received the chicks as an Easter gift from a former girlfriend. Apparently, they were cute at the time, but not a good gift for a college kid living in an apartment. His lease agreement explicitly stated, "NO CHICKENS OF ANY KIND ALLOWED!" I agreed to adopt the birdies out of pity for the broken-hearted friend. I understand the relationship ended abruptly.

All the chicks I purchased and the two I adopted turned out to be hens. Not a rooster in the lot. None of the chicks died along the way. I now have eggs, lots, and lots and lots of eggs. I'm sick of deviled eggs, scrambled eggs, over-easy eggs and every concoction that contains them. All my neighbors have eggs. I have an enormous chicken feed bill. I have lots of chicken manure. I have started a baker's dozen twelve-step program seeking help and I am seeing a fowl therapist. After thinking about the chickens for a long time, I circle back to my youthful days in Hondo. One of the things about visiting Grandma Diaz, the crazy lady with an axe, she made great fried chicken. It was the best.

# A Poem

## It Slips By

I'm going to miss my boy...
Our life is changing so drastically right now.
We have so many balls in the air that I cannot keep up.
We are looking at change in so many ways.


What can we do?
We cannot control what is happening around us.
It's like gamma radiation that slips through our bodies
affecting all of the tissues from skin to the marrow of bones.
Yet undetected, nary leaving a trace.

Our lives are changing.
Looking at my end and what legacy I leave.
Did I make my father proud?

I am going to miss him coming down in the morning
Pausing to greet me as I sit in the thinking chair…thinking.
I am going to miss him warming his legs and toes by the fireplace.
I am going to miss the opportunities to talk with him one on one.

I think about the many camping trips we never went on and the ones we did.

I am going to miss opening up the door to his room and finding it as it was.

H. Rodriguez
10/18/2018

# June 16, 1968

H WAS SLUMPED OVER AS HE GENTLY SHUFFLED TO THE suspended swing on the porch. His family often gathered on the front porch around the bench swing, el columpio, to talk about daily happenings, discuss problems, and relate family history, or just enjoy the calm of the evenings.

One of his grandsons was holding his hand, his finger really. The young boy was tugging the elder statesman along. At this time in his life, 82 years old, Papacito was tired, and his bones and joints had stiffened but his mind was still keenly alert. His hands were soft, and wisps of gray thinning hair stood fast to his head. He had a fresh haircut. "Oda si, Oda si" he whispered. Gold-rimmed spectacles sat gently on his nose. The old man had so much to do but what could be more important than this? Spending some time with a grandson with the hope he would be remembered. To be remembered would be nice he thought. But he was a realist and knew that time takes everyone down. "Who would remember me in 100 years?" "Will this young child ever tell my story?" he asked himself. The young boy was four years old and was different from other four-year-olds. The young lad was sitting with his grandfather, rocking on the front porch swing, looking at the old man making a memory and listening to the mourning doves as they cooed.

It was a steamy hot Texas afternoon. One that held humidity like the weight of a wet musty towel steamy. One of the old man's two sons was visiting from Austin. The son was a recently licensed attorney and married a young woman from the nearby town of Hondo. His son talked about the upcoming Supreme Court case that would prohibit racial discrimination in the housing rental markets across the United States. The old man felt he had done well and provided for his family, and most importantly, he provided for the education of his family. To him an education was the most important thing you could do for your family. He felt as though he accomplished this task. All his kids completed at least a four-year degree.

As the young attorney's family started to load up in the copper colored five-year-old Fury III station wagon, the old man made his way off the swing and porch. Shuffling his feet, the little four-year-old boy leading the way was pulling his grandfather by the finger. When the grandfather reached the car, he quietly passed his son a pad of paper about two inches thick and roughly five inches by seven inches, wrapped up in a piece of deep red cloth. It was a card stock and had holes punched in the upper right corner. The cards were attached with a metal loop like it was a series of flip cards. There must have been about a hundred of cards or so. The old man told his son that this was a narrative, handwritten notes, of some interesting portions of his life, his history. He told his son he would know what to do with it. His son thanked him, but he said he didn't have time to read it right now and promised he would. The old man smiled as the son drove away with his wife and three kids after a much too hurried weekend visit. The family was leaving for Puerto Rio in a few weeks. It was the next post assignment for the young military attorney. A melancholy feeling was welling up in the old man. The old man thought about it for a while. "That young boy will tell my story. He will remember. Would this be the last time I will see him and his family? The little one will remember me." he prayed. Papacito died in October of that year.

Papacito was my grandfather. My father's dad. I remember the card stock his life story was written on. I saw it once, but I have no idea where it is. The following is a translation into English by my father. He tried to keep the flavor and romance of Papacito words alive in the translation.

It's a very personal narrative, about a man with luck, character, and integrity. He was man with a sense of morals and compassion for others. From his humble beginning, the thirst for survival emerged and forged a man of character and a family man. He took everything life threw at him and lived to talk about it. He wrote his story because he could. He was educated. It is with great pride and yet great humility, I introduce you to Dr. Jose Simon Rodriguez M.D., born in Coahuila, Mexico in 1886.

## February 16, 1914

I do not want to leave among the shadows of forgetfulness those remembrances which I have always carried in my memory and for what reason I write theses lines. Which I cannot call an autobiography because not only do they lack the orderly literary format, but they also lack the picturesque and joyful details which adorn such a conversation. For this reason I have called these remembrances "a sincere family conversation" the objective of which is to talk to my children and relate to them how my lifetime developed to the present days to which the Lord has permitted me to reach the age of 71 years, from which peak I am now narrating all of the panorama which we all have written in the book of our remembrances.

So, therefore, with the only purpose being that my children, through these simple strokes of my pen, know the story as one lifetime which has nothing extraordinary other than that mutual particular interest which corresponds only to me and to my children. My life developed and evolved like many others which have episodes of semi-agitated youth and a tranquil serene maturity. This lifetime has not had those economic alternatives which sometimes bring about spiritual intranquilities nor those senseless acts, which at time accelerate the course of a lifetime. To the contrary, mine was a modest and humble lifetime which medicates the spirit and proportions to it a complete resignation to await peacefully the good as well as the bad. Mine was one of those lifetimes in which one does not think egotistically about those possessions of others with a desire to possess them. Never did I give thought to what others had so that I could also possess them; I could only think that if I ever were to have anything it would be only through my own efforts.

And so, with these thoughts and these illusions that nurtured my childhood spirit began the development of my lifetime in those first years. It was neither with the tenderness nor the loving caress of a mother who orders and dictates to her child with a kiss; nor was it with the comfort and wise counsel of a father who by his example indicates the way of life to a child's spirit as it starts at the threshold of a lifetime. None of this, all of this I never had. My mother died when I counted two years of age (1888) and my father, facing the impossibility of taking care and looking after me left me with my Aunt Antonia, my mothers' younger sister and with my maternal grandfather, Don Antonio Ramirez who was then remarried to a saintly lady whom I called "Mama".

However, to properly start this history, I must first refer you to some valuable documents (attached)which warrant examination and reading which are the marriage license of my parents, my baptismal certificate, and my birth certificate 1886.

So, there you have before you my parents which with pleasure I present to you as your grandparents. My father was a humble, modest, and decent man. My mother was, according to what I was told a devoted, loving, and saintly lady. From the marriage there were three offspring; a little girl, one year older than me who died a few months after birth; myself, who thanks to God has conserved me to this age and given me the opportunity to pass on this history to you; and another little girl a year younger than me who was also called to heaven a few months after birth.

As you see, I was the only survivor of that matrimony. I can just imagine how, with many denials and sacrifices, my dear Aunt Tona, an inexperienced maiden who then, herself, was totally dependent upon the protection of her father (my grandfather) who was then on his second marriage. At the side of these two dear beings, my infancy developed to the age of six (1892) years during which time they sent me to the village parochial school for a short period. A year later (1893), I was sent to the Public School where the Director was Don Diego Serrato. There I attended school until I completed the fourth year of primary instruction. At this point, a new parenthesis in my life developed. At 11 (1897) years of age and in view of the pressure of necessity to help with support of the home I commenced to work at hard field labors at the side of my Uncle Juan, my father's brother, who was then my Aunt Tona's husband. With such delight, I recall that it was necessary for my uncle and me to get up very early in the morning to go to work; it was not inconvenient for us to arise at four o'clock in the morning. We would then walk about 10 kilometers to arrive at the field where we worked at an early hour. We would then walk the same distance in the afternoon to be home at about six in the afternoon. At that age, one does not feel the fatigue of labor no matter how weary one may be. I would do this daily without hardly noticing and I did it gladly because I knew that it was necessary and expected to be done.

A very curious and unusual thing occurred at about that time. I counted on eleven years of age when on that occasion a relative of my uncle Juan, by the name of Onesimo Castro who lived nearby, arrived at the field where we were working. After the usual greetings, he asked my uncle if I knew how to read, write, and do arithmetic, to which my uncle answered in the affirmative because I had finished the fourth year of schooling. "That's good," he said to my uncle "because we are receiving a quantity of bricks for a construction and we need someone to count them when we receive them, and I believe we could use this boy to oversee this work." And so it was, the following day I started in my new task. After having noted, perhaps, my abilities as a "counter" of bricks, one fine day our relative confronted my uncle and said to him, "Say, Juan, this boy is very young to dedicate him to this hard field labor and what's more, he knows how to read and write, and he knows arithmetic, and it is not right to work him from sun-up to sun-down like all these illiterates. I have a compadre, Don Antonio B. Avila, who has a drug store in San Pedro, and I believe we could send the boy to him to use him in any way he could in the drug store. That way we would be able to get him out of this hard field labor which should not be for him. He is a bright lad, and it doesn't seem right to allow him to perhaps become ill in this fierce fun, as a field hand laborer."

And so it was, a few days later my life changed dramatically. I was no longer a hoe and shovel field hand and now I was a young humble servant boy in a drug store who most obediently did everything I was ordered to do. There before my eyes was a new world and panorama which made me think and dream of this new door which was opening new destinies in my life.

As to my father, he had remarried and was on his second nuptials when I was three years old, and he would only come to see me now and then. I first began to feel my solace when I was but eight years old, that is to say, feel the absence of my parents even though with my aunt and grandfather I had protection and support. I did not have the love and affection that I saw others my age had with their parents. I say this because I never knew what a parent's kiss or caress, or fondling was. I never had this. My grandfather was a good person but not really interested in me due to his occupation which absorbed all his days, and it was at night when he came home tired from his field hand work, he would talk about my Aunt Tona's complaints which were of course never kindly towards him.

I cannot say with any certainty that my behavior as a boy was good but I do know that my Aunt Tona's temper towards me was quite severe - to such an extent that at that young age I felt and knew that there existed no love of fondness for me here, that sooner or later I would have to make some radical change and that my destiny would obligate me to make such determination.

It would always bother my conscience if I were to, on the pretense of disclosure, leave the impression that my Aunt Tona was mean with me. No this is not so-never. She was a very strict character which would not allow me to have the distractions which are always so common among all children. But even so, I am grateful to her because in

135

this manner all of this was impressed in my mind and at times, I found the need to apply a replica of her strict character to the upbringing of my own children.

And so, time and the years moved on leaving behind in their paths those fixed recollections of a lifetime. I now counted thirteen years of age; it was 1898 when I started my occupation as a young servant boy and as a young clerk in the apothecary shop. Before long I had the distinction of being allowed to work for hours and times for days mixing with a pestle in a huge mortar the "azogue" or mercury with the liquid amber to prepare the double mercurial ointment. This task was one which took at least three weeks to a month to prepare.

In the passing of time as my services at the apothecary shop appeared to be greater usefulness because with dexterity and some agility, I could fold the paper medical containers and I could now manufacture or compound certain pills. My services were rendered at the apothecary shop for about one year without receiving any remuneration whatsoever; therefore, I believed that I was justified in manifesting my protest by running away to Torreon without telling anyone. A few days later my grandfather came looking for me and found me, but he could not convince me to continue working at the same place under the same conditions. On such occasion Senora Adel V. de Meave wife of Dr. Adolfo G. Meave also operated an apothecary shop in San Pedro, and they made me a proposition to enter their employment with a salary of six pesos per month. In addition to that salary, it was a matter of personal esteem and status for me. This created a feeling of responsibility, for which I labored honorably. I worked in this occupation for about a year, practically doing the work of a licensed apothecary because Dr. Meave, to some degree, trusted me to fill some of his prescriptions I was then approaching sixteen years of age-an age when juvenile aspirations and ambitious begin to awaken and I felt deep inside me the desire to do something with my life—to come out of this so very narrow and this rickety medium under which I was living. The youngsters, about my age, who every day passed in front of me, always so merry and joyful in a boisterous manner, with their books under their arms awakened a sadness and at times an envy because I was not able to attend school like they did. I would think much about this and form many fantasies which would awaken those daydreams where I could only see sketches of my hopes. "If only my family would have the possibilities," I would say to myself, "then they would be able to send me to school and I could finish my primary instruction and then they would send me to college and I would study to become a doctor, which is a beautiful profession" but my disillusion was even greater when I realized the sad situation, I was in.

Nonetheless, even though all these tempestuous clouds tortured my thoughts, they would at times blow away with the breezes of my optimism—all of the difficulties which always surrounded me. Mentally I would resolve them and somehow, I would place myself on the road to triumph and success. The first difficulty consisted of my lacking two years to complete my primary schooling but gathering all my courage I was determined to bring the matter up for consultation with my Aunt Tona and my Grandfather Antonio. Would I be allowed to live in their house and continue working and yet continue in schooling? After justified opposition to my plans, I succeeded in acquiring what I had desired, and I was also allowed to continue working in the same apothecary shop after school hours including Saturdays, Sundays and holidays. Now, that I had embraced my studies with much enthusiasm to a point that it caught the attention of my professors who gave me extra help so that I was able to complete my two years of primary schooling, which I was lacking, in one year. To this day I shall always be grateful for the kindness of my professors, Don Jesus Colunga in the fifth and Don Ladislao Covantes in the sixth who with their strength gave the moral support I needed, which I will never forget.

Upon completion of my primary instruction, I found myself with an enormous problem of continuing my studies in accordance with the plans which I had established. It was a terrible thought that to go to preparatory school, I would have to move to the city of Saltillo, the Capitol of the State, and I could not count on any resources, relatives or friends who would be able to lend me their support-moral or economical. After throwing to the wind this thought, I decided to look for a solution to my problem. So, I went to solicit the advice and counsel of my professor Don Ladislao Covantes who explained to me that the municipality maintained two scholarships to young students of limited resources who wanted to continue their studies. As quickly as possible, I went personally to see the Municipal President (Mayor) Don Andres Medellin, a very honorable and sensitive man who, after hearing all my reasons for the municipal scholarship, offered to present my case for consideration to the municipal governing body after he interviewed my professors. Surely the interviews with my teachers must have been favorable because the governing body at its next regular session approved my application and it was communicated to me that the municipality had conceded a monthly stipend of $12.50 pesos so that I could continue my schooling at the Prep School "Juan Antonio de la Fuente" known also as the "Ateneo (Athenaeum) Fuente" of Saltillo.

With my heart swollen with joy and hope and satisfied with my triumph, I communicated my determination to my relatives, who approved only in part because, justly so, they were of the opinion that a poor young boy, like myself, should not aspire or hope so much because I would not be able to count on support or help from anyone.

Regardless of all these justifiable objections, I could not abandon my purposes. Quite to the contrary, I gathered more enthusiasm, and decided to submit my problem to the consideration of Dr. Meave and his wife who initially were of the same opinion, that to say, that I was poor and that with so little help it would be impossible to sustain my preparatory studies. "Notwithstanding all of this," added Dr. Meave, "we will help you in any way possible." As time was slipping by rapidly and the date of my departure was approaching, I started making my preparations for the trip. Probably my enthusiasm and my determination awakened in Dr. Meave a feeling of sympathy towards me because quite spontaneously he offered to pay for my train fare and for a trunk for my belongings. Likewise, Mrs. Meave gave me a washbasin, a water pitcher, and a porcelain chamber pot. My clothing or wearing apparel was my problem and my family's. All these happenings were developing without the intervention or help of my father or any of my other relatives, which could have greatly helped me in those moments of need, but I could only count on the generous support of my Aunt Tona.

As all terms of time must arrive and all dates of time must be met, the date of my departure also arrived. "Who would be there to see me off?" "Who would be there to open their arms, embrace me, say 'Goodbye' and wish me well in my absence?" Only my Aunt Tona and my Cousin Margarita who shared my sadness with me and now shared the joyfulness of my trip. For the first time I would be abandoning the two that saw my birth and I would get to know the Villa of Torreon, a fantastically large city to me, a city where probably I would get lost because I knew no one who would serve as my guide. Even though I boarded the train with much enthusiasm, I also felt a great sadness in my soul because I was leaving behind all the remembrances of my childhood, my relatives and intimate school friends who shared with me the dawn of my youth, among whom I counted Antonio Farias, Jesus Cifuentes Uribe and Abellio Fernandez. Quickly that spiritual tempest passed, as did those sentimental farewell moments, which obscure the illusions of the future.

The deafening and monotonous noise of the railroad car invited boredom and my weariness nodded me to sleep until at last, at about 9:00 in the evening we arrived at the end of my journey, the City of Saltillo, the capitol of the state of Coahuila. After overcoming the difficulties, which are always encountered by a traveler to a strange place, I installed myself in the home of Dona Jesusita, a distant relative of Dr. Meave, from whom I had a letter of introduction, since she had a rooming house for students. Although it seemed different awakening in a strange house, I felt a gaiety in a youthful atmosphere, for I found that three other boys who were also from my hometown were rooming there, Ernesto Salas, Panchito Gonzalez and Jesus Alcoa.

At the present time during which I am writing this (1957), only with great effort of the imagination is it possible to understand this fact. At that time, in 1904, I paid $12.50 (pesos) monthly for my room, candles for light, and three meals a day which is exactly what I received as a stipend from the municipality. The remainder of my general expenses I paid with my work which was early in the morning in the judicial offices where they paid me 25 centavos for each page I would copy.

Thus, passed my first year of preparatory school from 1904 to 1905. Upon completion of my courses, it was my good fortune to receive The First Place Standing in Mathematics and in National Language courses and Honorable Mention in the Lineal Drawings Course. While this was happening, Mrs. Meave was writing to me to offer me my train fare to return home if I would work in their drug store during my two months' vacation.

I could not afford to lose this magnificent opportunity and thereupon I immediately accepted their proposition. My vacation plans being firmed up, Mrs. Meave then granted me five ($5.00) pesos per month so that I could cover the remainder of my school expenses. Now I felt that decisively the door of my good fortune was opening so that I could begin to plan my second school year. Even though I did not receive first place standings I did make good grades. Once again vacation time came and this year, I took advantage of them by working in the Foundry of

Saltillo. My savings from this enabled me the pleasure of taking an adventure trip to Mexico City with my school companion, Francisco de P. Berlingo who I fondly called "Compadre". It would take too long to talk about the adventures on this trip: suffice it to say that we made it without the fare costing us hardly anything. To solve the matter of our college expenses for the third year my "Compadre" and I started two school newspapers, one "The Ray" and the other "La Alborada", in English "The Twilight". At the beginning of classes of the fourth year there was a contest for the winner to serve as an assistant in the physics and chemistry department. I entered the contest, and it was my good fortune to be the winner. This assistant position had a salary of twenty ($20.00) pesos per month which added to my scholarship stipend gave me the neat sum of $32.50 pesos per month which I could comfortably live and clothe myself in a manner corresponding to a senior student in the city of Saltillo. I now had the basis with which to support myself and complete my last year of preparatory schooling, so now it no longer a difficult problem for me to resolve.

Nevertheless, upon terminating that school year an unknown would come upon me which be difficult to resolve. What was I going to do? Would I be able to move to Mexico City—the capitol—to enroll myself in the National School of Medicine which was my ideal? I did not know how-nor any idea entered my imagination which

143

could give me any hope. The only thing I knew was that in some manner I would enter this career.

What we call good luck of persons is nothing more than the reflection of their good conduct. My conduct as a student had always been good perhaps due to this circumstance there came about what I referred to as my good luck. Final exams were near, and I would be completing my preparatory schooling. Although I had various projects in mind none of them gave me any certainty. One day, when I least expected it, I received an appointment notice from the Director of the School, Sr. Don Jose Garcia Rodriguez, a very cultured person, and distinguished poet who was very highly regarded by the then Governor of the State, Lic. Miguel Cardenas. That appointment notice came to me as a great surprise, and it made me think immediately of something wrong I may have done. "Rodriguez" the Director said to me, "you are about to terminate your studies in this school, do you plan to study some career? Since you are a good young man and according to the information I have, you do not have the means to do so, I have been observing you in order to ask the Governor of the State to grant you a scholarship so that you may continue your schooling in Mexico City. If my request is granted and you know how to respond by your dedication to your studies, the State will feel satisfied in having complied with a duty by placing their confidence in you. So, return to this office in one week and I will inform you of the results of my request to the Governor. Prepare your studies well so that you will not fail in your final exams. I hope you do well." So intense was the impression upon me by that notice given by the Director of the School that I became confused to the point that I did not know how to express my gratefulness for what he was doing for me without having even requested it. That afternoon when I returned to my room, I lay down on my bed with my head buried under my pillow to try to recapture and savor those moments of happiness. When the week was complete, I anxiously returned to receive the desired response from the Director which was most favorable in the full sense of the word because the Governor had granted me a scholarship of $125.00 pesos per month so that I might enroll in the School of Medicine.

Upon completing my fifth and final year of preparatory school, I returned to the town of my birth taking with me the sincere pleasure of my good news to my relatives and to Dr. Meave and his wife.

During the middle of 1909 I undertook my journey with my school companion Jesus Valdes Cardenas who was enrolling in the School of Mining to study the career of Civil Engineering. I enrolled in the National School of Medicine without any difficulty because all my documents were in perfect order.

That very ancient building, which had been the seat of the Inquisition, presented itself to be most imposing with all its historic background in my eyes as a provincial student. In the corridors of the great patio of the building there was a blackboard which was used to post the official notices for the students and the date was made known when classes were to start and so that each student would make note of the place where he was to go. On opening day of classes, a typical student incident, which I later considered quite funny, occurred to me and I will now relate it in the manner I told it many years later during a special occasion. It goes like this; In the year 1909 a motley but resolved group of lads coming from different parts of the country entered upon the threshold of the very ancient building of the Inquisition to inscribe themselves as students in the National School of Medicine of the Mexican Capitol.

I find it impossible to separate in my mind the memories of that day of the beginning of classes because I consider it to be prologue to the book of my remembrances of the School of Medicine. Already lined up along the ample corridors of the large central patio of the school were the upper-class students who were awaiting the proper moment to baptize with traditional teasing the arriving new students for whom they had nary a smile but a jeering laugh, as well as challenging stares of curiosity. It was truly imposing to see all the student body with the humor appropriate for their age attending the parade of novices who with their provincial modesty noted their walk and their dress presented the most charmingly colorful spectacle that may be imagined. Even now my memory holds that very special image of northern youngsters with their loose-fitting trousers tightly girdled below their waist and their bright colorful suited jacket with flaps reaching to their thighs.

I now recall with great relish something that happened to me at that time. Since my means were very limited and I considered myself quite elegantly dressed with my cashmere trousers and yellow alpaca jacket, it seemed correct to me to make my triumphant entrance to the medical school wearing this apparel. Never had I ever been the object of so much applause and cheers as I had on this occasion. I would have very much have wanted, as is commonly said, that the earth would have opened and swallowed me during those moments. One thing, though, that innocent attire of clothing which brought me much applause on that memorable first day, was sentenced, from that moment on to spend the rest of its existence in the pawn shop, unless someone, unbeknownst to me had compassion on it.

As time passed, all of us provincial students became familiar with the way of life in the capital city and its customs. The surprises for us occur each day and thus is how on this my first year as a student, 1910, with great admiration I was able to witness the grand festivities of the first centennial of Mexican independence presided over by the great national personage of General Don Porfirio Diaz. Very frequently he would be seen parading by without formal escorts accompanied by his ministers down the street then known as "Calle de Plateron" and today named "Francisco I. Madero." The great parades were made, in those days on sumptuous carriages pulled by beautiful horses. One would have to see to truly admire the robust figure of the President of the Mexican Nation who, in simply traveling the road from Castle of Chapultepec where he lived to the National Palace, he was the motive of great admiration and reverence. In the midst of this grand parade of popular manifestations and rejoicing I completed my first year of medical school. Notwithstanding all of this, about the middle of my second year, the irregularity in the payment of the scholarship which I had been granted by my home state began. This was due to the political tension which was being manifested at all social spheres throughout the country.

These circumstances caused me to look for new economic horizons which would enable me to complete my second scholastic year. I then started performing the duties of a practicing apprentice commissariat in charge of the Tacubaya General Hospital admissions and a short time later I was also an apprentice practitioner at the hospital for demented women located in those years on the Calle de Donceles in front of the Chamber of Deputies. With these two salaries I amply fulfilled my student expenses and there was no longer any disorder in my scholastic routine, therefore I was not affected when my monthly stipend was suspended due to the great revolutionary and political agitation in my home state. Since the politico-revolutionary agitation now extended to nearly all parts of the country the communications were now very irregular I lost nearly all contact with my family and Dr. Meave's family. As a gesture of my genuine sincerity, I took advantage of the first opportunity to extend to Dr. and Mrs. Meave my thanks for their help since I now considered my economic condition sufficient to enable me to support myself.

At the commencement of my third year of medical school (1911 to 1912) I solicited for entry to the Military Medical School where I was accepted initially with the rank of common soldier (practicing medical apprentice) and a few months later with the rank of Sub-Lieutenant Aspirant in Medicine with a salary of $90.00 pesos per month. Since my military commitments did not interfere with my studies in the National School of Medicine the rhythm of my studies did not suffer any transformation, I continued attending my classes and clinics in the same manner as before and only my services as apprentice practitioner were now performed at the Military Instructional Hospital which at the time was located at the Calle de Cacahuatal, being practically back-to-back with the Juarez Hospital which is still located at this place.

A few months after being given the rank of Sub-Lieutenant, I was ordered on a mission to render my services at Guaymas, Sonora, together with four fellow medical students, a Lieutenant whose name escapes my memory, Sub-Lieutenant Pedro Perez Gravas, Sub-Lieutenant Guadalupe Jimenez and Sub-Lieutenant Ricardo Alvarez. We made the trip to and from the Port of Manzanillo by train and from there to Guaymas on a National Government ship. We remained on this mission about a month and a half subject to the orders of the general headquarters of that city. My fourth year of Medical School developed from 1912 to 1913 and the political-revolutionary events were occurring throughout the country with great dread. All lines of communication were destroyed in most of the country and a constant movement of civil and military nature were now being observed in all official circles. These events culminated with the unforgettable Tragic Ten of the Capital, Decena Tragica de la Capital which terminated with the repugnant apprehension and death of the President of the Republic Don Francisco I. Madero. My status as a military-student obligated me during the days the National Palace was under attack to remain on duty at the Military Instructional Hospital. Because this deals with an episode of my life as a student and in addition being an interesting historical fact, I will narrate it here in a manner which I did so on a previous intimate reunion of friends, and I then entitled this:

# "A Historical Narration"

It was during those unfortunate days of the Tragic Ten, in the City of Mexico in which the whole country, shaken by the awesome political happenings, was awaiting a solution which would bring an end to that painful situation. During the afternoon of the 18th of February of 1913, a telephone call placed into action all of the medical personnel on duty at the Military Instructional Hospital, situated in those days on the Calla de Cachuatal in the City of Mexico. From the National Palace there was an urgent request for an ambulance with attending personnel to transport two seriously wounded persons whose condition required immediate attention. As soon as the ambulance returned to the hospital, we found that there were in fact two wounded, one civilian, the other a military man with the rank of sergeant.

Immediately, the medical orders were given respectively for the wounded persons to be taken to the operating rooms so that they may be given the necessary medico-surgical attention. The personnel to assist in each were designated since both cases involved wounds penetrating the abdomen which had been caused by a projectile from firearms. Since I was an advanced pasante medical student with the rank of Sub-lieutenant I was a witness to and present during a surgical procedure performed on the wounded civilian. The personnel in charge of performing that operation consisted of Lieutenant Colonel Medical

Corps, Fructoso Trigoyen, Major Medical Corps, Samuel Silva, and a Lieutenant—Practitioner whose name escapes my memory but who we affectionately called "Suchil." A medium caparotomy was preformed to arrive at the cause of the wound penetrating into the abdomen, the cause projectile from a firearm, which produced the perforation and tearing of the peritoneum as well as various intestinal vaults, all of which thereupon made one think of an immediate fatal prognosis due to the profound state of shock of the patient. When about finished with the surgical procedure, the neophyte Lieutenant called Dr. Silva's attention to a solid body that was within the intestinal mass. And effectively so, Dr. Silva proceeded with utmost care to extract the foreign body, which was no less than a silver coin, of Mexican mintage, of one peso, which apparently the wounded man had had in his vest pocket and which the bullet pushed into his abdomen. This coin caused all the tearing up on the peritoneum and the intestines which had been found when performing the surgical procedure. The patient died after the surgical intervention was terminated.

Now comes the historical part of this event. While President Madero was being apprehended in the National Palace, firearms were discharged, wounding the already mentioned Sergeant. Marco Hernandez, a a civil engineer and a relative of Mr. Madero, was also wounded when he moved between Mr. Madero and the apprehenders and took the bullet that would otherwise have struck the President. The projectile directly hit a coin in one of the pockets of Mr. Hernandez's vest and pushed the coin into Mr. Hernandez's abdomen. Since Mr. Hernandez's coin impeded the bullet and prevented Mr. Madero from a possible wound or even his death, it can be said that the coin saved the life of the President.

As time passed, as did many revolutionary events relevant to public order, the said Dr. Silva who had kept the coin, was ordered to duty to the northern part of the country where due to some special circumstances of the moment he had been captured and was a prisoner of the Villista forces. He, together with other military persons, had been all given a death sentence by General Pancho Villa himself. While being conducted on a military train to a determined location to be brought before a firing squad, Dr. Silva had the opportunity to come in contact with the Military Medical Officer of the Villista forces and he then had the opportunity to communicate to him the critical circumstances in which he found himself, and since it was a matter of his life he implored that he interpose all of his influence with the end of saving him from the firing squad. Possibly with the objective of influencing him in his behalf he offered to the Villista Medical Officer the special coin and narrating to him the history it contained and why he (Dr. Silva) had it in his possession. Whether or not this historical narration influenced the Villista Medical Officer, the fact of the matter is that Dr. Silva found an opportunity to escape from the train he was on and thus saved himself from facing the firing squad. It could be said that the relation of the history contained in that coin greatly influenced the Villista doctor who then found a way to facilitate Dr. Silva's escape. On this occasion one could consider that the coin also saved the life of Dr. Silva.

Later, I have learned that this historical coin was offered to General Villa so that he might possess it and apparently today no one knows for certain in whose possession it is so that it may be safeguarded as a historical relic of great value to posterity. Truthfully, that coin, with just cause, may be said to have in fact saved two lives, those of President Madero and of Dr. Silva.

After the passing of the political agitation which culminated in the death of President Don Franciso I. Madero and Mr. Jose Maria Pino Suarez, Vice President, the political events followed in the historical form already known. This was followed by the military movement led by the Governor of the State of Coahuila, Don Venustiano Carranza, who expressed with his rebellious attitude the general mood of the rest of the country, not being in conformity with the assassination of the President and Vice-President of the Republic.

Although my position was that of a spectator and my commitments as a student obligated me to remain silent and on the edge of these events, nevertheless, these assassinations disrupted my tranquility, and I overcame my desire and impulse of rebellion only because of my being so close to the termination of studies and my graduation. This was the situation and during such turbulent political rebellion I continued my studies until the middle of 1914. About a month before the definitive triumph of the Constitutional Army I was finishing my school year and my studies in Medical School. During the first days of the month of August of 1914 I was assigned the subject for my professional thesis which was to write upon the suppurating (generating pus) Mastoiditis and the surgical treatment thereof with the trephination of the prominent part of the mastoid.

In the midst of all the intranquility which spread over all social classes throughout the country as well as into the student classes which were already indirectly participating in the Revolutionary movements, I prepared and presented my professional exam and my thesis. An uncontainable spiritual intranquility fluttered within me during those moments which seemed to me more like years and condensed all my illusions and hopes of my life that upon receiving my title from The National University of Mexico that I be accredited as a medical doctor, a surgeon, and obstetrician. The day of the culmination of this arrived at the moment that the Secretary of the Certifications Panel extended his hand to give me a sealed envelope which with anxiety and despondency I opened in the midst of a group of on-looking classmates who accompanied me with tears in their eyes while I read aloud that saving sentence which stated to the letter:

To <u>Student Simon Rodriguez</u>:

In the General Examination of Medicine of Medical, Surgery, and Obstetrics which you have undertaken in this School and which you terminate on this day, the jury was kind enough to approve you unanimously. I now communicate for your understanding in compliance with the disposition of the Regulations of this school. Mexico, 25th of August of 1914.

The Secretary
Dr. Rafael Rojas Loa

The culminating event was to take place at 6:00 in the afternoon. We all ran to my room which was located on the Calle de la Moneda where my accompanying friends congratulated me, lit some Stearine candles, and with all dissipation of their economic resources at that moment they opened some bottled beer to toast my triumph.

The next day how different was my awakening. I was now a medical doctor and had terminated my function as an apprentice practitioner, and with this my salary terminated. Thereupon, I immediately requested my diploma from the Secretariat of Instruction with Fine Arts and from the Department of Public Health my corresponding registration. With the date of 22nd of September of 1914 I received the diploma which publicly vested my credentials as a Medical Doctor, Surgeon, and Obstetrician legally authorizing me to practice my profession.

We must recall, I was or that I belonged to the Military School attached to the Federal Army; but by coincidence it happened that during those days by a Presidential decree there was a total discharge of all the Army so in that release I was included; therefore, all of my obligations automatically ended including the two years I was to serve the Federal Government. By this time, the Constitutionalist System had begun presided over by the Commander in Chief, Don Venustiano Carranza and I then decided to affiliate myself with the Revolutionary Party and I entered the Medical Services in the forces commanded by General Jesus Davila Sanchez with the rank of Major, in the medical corps. This happened during the month of October 1914.

# A NEW ODYSSEY

Since the triumph of Constitutionalism did not bring about the end to the political agitation and the merits thereof were being opposed by the Carrancismo and Villismo ideologies there came about a new partitioning. The forces to which I now belonged found themselves obligated to move from the Capitol towards Toluca during the month of November to join with a Division under the command of the then Governor and Commander of the State of Mexico, General Francisco Murgia who was Chief of Staff under General Arnulfo Gonzalez my old friend and classmate from college in Saltillo, Coahuila. During our travel towards Toluca, we were attacked by another military fraction that was not in accord with us, the Zapatistas. This attack took place at El Monte de Las Cruces, beginning precisely at the portion of the convoy where the Medical Section I was commanding, was located. This section consisted of myself as the medical commander, a Lieutenant-Practicing named Jesus Gomez, a Sub-Lieutenant named Alfonso Perales-Vega and six soldiers who were male nurses. Our convoy section was equipped with two utility wagons each towed by six mules. In these wagons we transported medical materials including surgical instruments, stretchers, and medicines to the front of our section; as van guard mounted on horseback was Lieutenant Jesus

Gomez and in the second wagon were Sub-Lieutenant Perales Vega and me. During the surprise attack one of the first wagons to stop was the one I was traveling in due to one of our mules having been killed. Now being obligated to descend from the wagon we also noticed that Lieutenant Gomez had been killed by a bullet that struck his head. Since firing was increasing every moment Sub-Lieutenant Perales Vega and I found ourselves obligated to seek refuge in the undergrowth, ready to defend our lives as may be necessary. When the skirmish was over, with great difficulty, we came out on the road where having been seen by the enemy, they tried to finish us off also. To our good fortune, we came out of this unharmed and with two prisoners whom we disarmed and turned over to our prisoner section. We continued our advance towards Toluca where we replaced our losses and continued on the road towards Morelia, Michoacán.

A little before arriving at the City of Morelia our column was detained because the Governor of the State was on the side of Villesmo and would not permit our entry into the city. The Governor was Coahuilan General Gertrudis G. Sanchez, and the Chief of Staff was Colonel Joaquin Amaro. Finally, after a conference between General Francisco Murgia, Commander of our troops and General Sanchez, Governor of the State, we were able to enter the city. The conference took place in the town of Charro after which it was possible to enter the city of Morelia in a peaceful manner. We remained in the city for a few days after which we continued our march towards the State of Jalisco where the governor and Military Commander was General Manuel M. Dieguez. On the day that we were leaving the city of Morelia General Gertrudis G. Sanchez was absent from the Charro pact convention. For this reason, they detained in the city the rear guard of the convoy which included the Medical Section I was commanding. We were retained in the city, and we were assigned to serve in the Military Hospital. In the city I found many men (paisanos) from my home state who were followers of General Gertrudis G. Sanchez viz., serving as counselor and advisor to the general was Lic. Gustavo Figueroa: my compadre Francisco de P. Berlanga, alias "El Camaleno," a Captain Melchor Cardenas and a fellow named Padilla, all from Saltillo and old friends of mine. Thereupon, due to the friendships of these "paisanos" from my home state with the Governor I was named Director of the Military Hospital. It was there I met medical students, Manuel Baez, Adolfo Arreguim, and Arturo Rascon who placed themselves under my orders and in whose presence, I performed an amputation of an arm at the shoulder joint at this Military Hospital. Two weeks later the wave of politics obligated General Sanchez to abandon the city and march with his forces to the south. On this march we arrived at Tacambaro where our forces sustained a heavy encounter with the forces under the command of

Generals Renteria-Luvuno and Mastache formerly subordinates of General Sanchez. All the command staff, among them myself were accompanying the Commander in the Chief General Gertrudis G. Sanchez and we were observing the combat from nearby hills right in the midst of the resounding noises of the fusillades, the machine gun fire and the cannons. By surprise and in the darkness of night we heard some enemy machine gun fire to the rear of our group. Since this turned out to be an unexpected attack, confusion took possession of us, and a yell was heard "Each on his own! Save yourself if you can!"

I was mounting a spirited horse and upon hearing the detonations the horse rose on his hind feet and slipped down a small canyon. Upon falling to the bottom of the small canyon I lost track of my mount and in the darkness, I tried only to find some refuge. After the confusion subsided somewhat, I tried climbing to find a way out. Since every few moments I would hear noises in the confusion, I tried to locate some companion and I then used a whistling countersignal which my compadre "Camaleno" and I interpreted to say in the whistle "Where are you?—Where are you?—Where are you?—I cannot see you?" It was truly a surprise to hear a whistling in response to my signal which could come from no one except my compadre. And so, it was that we reunited and started to walk in the darkness without knowing where and taking all necessary precautions called for. Along the bottom of a creek bed, we walked all night and as it was dawning, we heard the noise of someone who was following us and sure enough it was a man whose last name was Chavez who was a member of our forces. He gave us the notice that General Sanchez had been wounded and that they urgently needed my services. 'Climb out of this creek bed" he told us "And take to your left. Go about two kilometer and there you will find some of our advanced forces, identify yourselves and a short distance from that point you will come upon Caracara, where General Sanchez is to be found in urgent need of medical services".

My compadre Berlanga separated from us to continue moving on. Taking the precautions called for, a young man by the name of Padilla and I made contact with the advanced forces, and they indicated to us the road we should follow to find the General. I immediately proceeded to give him first aid. The injury consisted of an angling bullet wound with the entry aperture at the right elbow and the exit aperture at the flex or cutaneous frontal crease of the elbow with laceration of the skin tissue in the region. Upon completing the treatment as darkness came upon us, we once again started our march in a southerly direction with General Jose Innocents Lugo taking command of the column. He knew the region of the State of Guerrero. We traveled all night to arrive at the summit of the mountain where we stayed for the remainder of a very restless night because we knew the enemy was following us. It was there that the General was once again treated, and we found that the wound was now infected.

At dawn we renewed our march, but it became necessary to transport our wounded patient in a stretcher. At about 8:00 in the morning the enemy attacked us, dispersed our column, and took General Gertrudis G. Sanchez prisoner. They took him to their general headquarters at Huetamo where without any consideration whatsoever, they had the intrepidity of shooting him while in the stretcher. Thus, at the hands of his own subordinates, Generals Pantoja-Mastache and Renteria-Luviano, ended the life of a good Revolutionary who greatly contributed to the final triumph of the revolutionary cause. While this was happening a group of us dispersed troops joined with General Jose Innocents Lugo to continue our march towards the coast of the State of Guerrero. On this same day at evening time, we were pursued and attacked by a Zapatista patrol. During the confusion and protected only by darkness we became isolated and not knowing where we were, Sub-Lieutenant Alfonso Perales and I started walking without course until dawn when we were apprehended and made prisoners by a group of about 20 Zapatistas. We were then conducted to a place nearby where they, not wanting to lose time in the pursuit of the rest of our column, ordered our execution by firing squad. We were placed against a wall in front of five soldiers and as the order "Ready, Aim, fire was about to be given, by a true miracle, the Zapatista commander suspended the order and moved towards me to interrogate me. "If you are a doctor and your companion is your assistant, how do you prove it?"

"At this moment it would be impossible for me to do so," I told him, "I have only on hand these few sheets from my prescription pad." After the secretary read one of the sheets to him the commander ordered the firing squad execution suspended while they decided my fate. Those blessed sheets from my prescription pad saved my life for the moment.

The death sentence was withdrawn and still in a prisoner status the order was given that our hands be bound behind our backs, and we be made to march along with a line tied to us held by a soldier mounted on a mule. We were then obligated to march along with them while they pursued the rest of our troops.

We barely left one adversity and entered another. By now we had passed twenty-four hours without drinking water or tasting any food. We felt our strength was failing us and materially it was becoming impossible for us to continue on foot at the same pace of those who were mounted. In a state of intense physical and moral torture I was now comprehending that the moment arrived to make resolution and I then thought that death would be better than this martyrdom. I felt weakening and faint and told my custodian: "I cannot go on-do with me whatever you want. I cannot walk anymore." Surely, the picture I presented must have been a moving one because that rough soldier stopped and handed me a bottle of Mescal and said: "Take this, friend, and drink what you want so that you can walk." With great despair I took the bottle and drank nearly half of it, I felt restored and said to him: "I'm ready for whatever you want." We then continued to march and after walking for a while we came upon a cabin where a true hermit lived. He was an older man with a long beard, with long rough hair, very dirty clothing which was ragged and torn. Our guards moved close to him and the one in charge placed us under his total responsibility. In our condition heavy with sleep, we were made to enter the only hut, and the hermit pointed to the only bed to us for us to rest upon. The bed was a wide wooden frame with woven wide strips of leather which in that part of the country is called a "canchiri". "You may rest there." he told us. The enemy soldiers continued their march past the hut when suddenly a soldier who had been drinking came to the entry way of the hut and upon seeing us stretched out on the bed, he exclaimed: "We might as well finish them off instead of having to carry them along with us." At the same time, he grasped a pistol with his right hand and with his left a huge dagger. He was determined to finish us off as we lay defenseless on the bed. Upon noticing the attempted assault, the hermit jumped like a furious tiger and grabbed a Mauser rifle he kept behind the door, quickly chambered a round, and standing in front of the soldier who was lunging at us and said "Before allowing a crime to be committed in my house, I will kill you, now get back! The chief turned them over to me alive and I will return them to him alive, now get on your way if you don't want to be killed!" Since the rife was much more eloquent than his words, the soldier did an about face and was on his way. Once again, our lives had been saved.

Late that afternoon the Zapatista Chief returned with all his soldiers, and he ordered that we be brought before him so that they could turn over to us a wounded woman whom the carried on a makeshift stretcher. "That wounded woman was the companion of one of our officers and I want to be convinced," said the Zapatista Chief, directing himself to me, "whether or not you are a doctor. Here is this wounded woman: take charge of her, and I want you to know if she is saved, I will set you free, but if she dies, then you also die." I then proceeded to examine he and I noted that the woman was in grave condition. She had an angling wound produced by a projectile from a firearm with an entry aperture at the hepatic region of the liver and the exit aperture located at the back. According to the information I was given the officer and the woman were traveling together on a mule, he in front and the woman behind him. The same projectile had killed the officer instantly and she had been picked up in a grievous state.

The sentence the Zapatista Chief had given was firm, severe, and decisively applicable to me. At that remote place I had no means by which to procure medication for the woman upon whose life mine was dependent. How could I do something for that wounded woman at this place where I had no medication or equipment whatsoever? I asked for a bottle of Mescal and with this I moistened some pieces of linen they had found for me with some difficulty, then with these I placed an external application on the entry and exit apertures and thus I completed the first treatment of the patient there in the field.

Later that night we arrived at the cottage where they had their general headquarters. They placed the wounded woman in a hut where some of the ranch people were housed and they placed us, Sub-Lieutenant Perales Vega, and me, in another hut with sentinels at the door. With a little more consideration, they gave us some supper-some roast meat and warm corn tortillas-which seemed like a feast to us considering the proportion of our appetite.

We rested that night and at daybreak they took us to the place where the wounded woman was housed. I found her, to my great joy, much better, and her general condition was encouraging with some hope that she could be saved. Since I only had the same medication material I had before I proceeded to change the dressings for some clean ones of the same kind. Upon making my visit the next day I found, to my great surprise, that the woman had escaped which made me suppose two things; that the patient's condition had improved considerably, and that the people around her and took care of her helped her to escape. These events strengthened my spirit and made me think about our liberty. From that time on they removed our daily sentinels and imposed upon us as our place of confinement that separate cottage where they originally had their general headquarters. There, every night in front of a small fire, we were surrounded by our captors listening to our conversations which seemed to them to be fantastic and pleasant because we adorned the conversations with the eloquence at our command. Our topics covered such things as the round shape of our world, eclipses, electrical discharges, and navigation. In those distant places where we were prisoners, all the men and women formed an intimate fondness towards us to the extent that they carried their influence to their Chief who then started thinking about our liberty but at the same time not forgetting his own responsibilities, bearing in mind that we were his prisoners.

His military problem quickly presented itself. The superior military authorities, of course, ordered that we be sent forward to them; but this chief feared for our lives because for certain we would be considered as dangerous leaders. At the same time, he had to consider the responsibilities he would encounter if he were to set us free and facilitate our escape. Close to that vicinity lived a man of German nationality who was very well liked and highly respected by all in the area. This man was involved in mining exploration activities and for this reason was well known by all. The Zapatista Chiefs had a good idea of sending him a messenger with a special letter setting forth our case and requesting his good counsel to resolve that problem which in summary was as follows: If he were to set us free or facilitates our escape, he would be assuming the military consequences and if he was to deliver us to higher headquarters he feared for our lives. He did not have to wait long for a response which was the following. He was to choose some soldiers in whom he had complete confidence and trust and send us forward with them, making sure that they would in their possession have his official delivery orders. He was to make arrangements with a trusted friend in the region to send us so that we could be delivered the German miner. After delivering us to the trusted friend the soldiers would continue on their way and give the official delivery orders to the superior chief with whom they would be safeguarded and insofar as the prisoners were concerned they were to explain that they had escaped, and therefore we would be saved from another attempt on our lives.

And so, it happened, and it turned out as planned. The person to whom we had been sent manifested satisfaction not only in being able to receive us but also in being able to do something to help save us. This man was a Protestant Minister and of course he presented us to his parishioners who started saying daily prayers to the Almighty that he might help us to come out of that dangerous situation.

The day after our arrival we received notice to the effect that some groups of Zapatistas were marauding in the area and our protector, the minister, in order to keep us safe, conducted us to a safe hideout from which we were to come out to receive our food and water only on an agreed signal. After the danger passed, this kind man contacted one of his parishioners who lived with his family at the summit of the mountain known as Argelia in the State of Guerrero. As soon as he received a response, he had us led to the parishioner by persons whom he trusted. This parishioner, who seemed hermit-like to us due to his long and heavy beard, made his living, together with his family, by growing wheat. He had two sons who were light skinned and husky who helped him with his work. Several days after our arrival this man organized a trip to the coast of Guerrero to sell, by barter, his harvest of wheat. We, who were also light complected, could also pass for his sons and could help him conduct the herd of 20 burros loaded with sacks of wheat. Of course, we changed from our wearing apparel for white muslin pantaloons and over shirts, sandals called huaraches and a huaripa or straw hat in order to appear to be part of his family. It would take us about two days to get down the mountain where the family lived.

Our first night we made our camp at a place which had a pond like swamp. Once we were settled, we performed the chores of helping unload the sacks of wheat and formed a corral with them within which we spent the night. Upon finishing this task, they explained to us that about one half kilometer away there was a spring of good drinking water where we would half to go to resupply our water before darkness because after dark it was dangerous due to wild beasts such as mountain lions and wild javalina. Having concluded this task and enclosing the burros in the corral, we then took turns over the night guarding from wild animal attack.

Dawn was beginning to break when we started the task of loading the cargo on the burros so we could continue our journey. Later afternoon of the same day we arrived at a town named Villa Union in the State of Guerrero. We were to be introduced to the town druggist for whom we had a letter of recommendation from our protector already mentioned, the Protestant Minister. The druggist, after reading the letter asked us where the doctors referenced in the letter were to be found. He could not imagine that those being recommended to him were being presenting themselves in muslin pantaloons and unbleached cotton shirts, sandals, and straw hats. After explaining to him the reason for our wearing such attire, after being reassured, he offered that, of course we would be furnished with some shirts made from the only color fabric to be found in the whole town, a pale green. We were also provided some appropriate trousers, brown shoes, and small brim straw hats. Knowing full well that our stay at that location was dangerous, he then proceeded to furnish us with two horses and gave us a letter of recommendation for a friend of who at that time was the Chief of the Port of Zihuantanejo, Guerrero. He explained to us that it would be unnecessary for someone to accompany us and therefore he only gave us directions on how to get there and said it would take two hours to get there. We were well received by the Chief of the Port of Zihuantanejo, and he offered us meals and lodging until we could continue our journey to the Port of Acapulco. Zihuantanejo was a coastal-trading port where only sailing vessels of low draught would arrive now and then. A whole month passed without the port being visited by some ship of the kind that occasionally did so trade their merchandise and cargo of primary necessities for furs of all kinds. Since we were under the protection of the aforesaid Chief of the Port, when he received word that the armed forces were nearby, as a precaution he would put us on a launch and would direct us to some nearby safe place where we could spend the night without fear of being surprised. At last, on a fine day notice was given that a sailing ship of the type that now visited that place was sighted coming in on a commercial visit. We made arrangements with the captain of the cargo ship to transport us to the Port of Acapulco when suddenly a steamer of great tonnage was sighted approaching the harbor to take on fresh water. As such great opportunity opened to us, we decided to leave the sailing ship and transfer to the steamer, which was of British Registry, by the name of "NARROW." After making the necessary arrangements with the captain we freighted on board his ship and the following day we disembarked at the Port of Acapulco. After arriving at this port, we made arrangements with the same vessel to continue our journey to the Port of Salinas Cruz. We remained a few days at this port and then decided to make some other plans and determinations. My companion in these adventures, Alfonso Perales Vega, was to continue his journey to Oaxaca and I would remain in the City of Tehuantepec practicing my profession in order accrue some funds. Then I was to continue my journey to Veracruz, a place where it was certain that the national forces were located under the command of the primary Chief Don Venustiano Carranza.

I remained in Tehuantepec about one month and had it not been for an attack of Malaria, which struck me, I found myself in need of leaving this picturesque place with all its varied attractions and different customs such as the special manner of dressing. I then boarded the Isthmus Railroad train to travel towards the Port of Coatzacoalcos, now known as the Port of Mexico. While there I was able to see and admire marvelous mouth of the Coatzacoalcos River. After having remained there for two days I then boarded the Mexican ship "COAHUILA" and arrived three days later at the Port of Veracruz. It was there I met up with many of my friends and companions who were with our National Commander Chief Don Venustiano Carranza. Among such persons were notables as Lic. Able Barragan, also from Saltillo who was the Sub-National Treasurer General and principal assistant to Mr. Niceforo Zamorano of Monterrey who was the National Treasurer. The next day after my arrival in Veracruz at the invitation of some of my countrymen at mid-day I visited the gathering place Coahuilans called "Babaria" situated at Portales. It was there I greeted the Treasurer General of the nation, my amiable and fine friend Mr. Able Barragan who in addition to having given me a hearty welcome also offered me his services if I were to need them.

My stay in Tehuantepec, Oaxaca permitted me to save some $5000.00 constitutional pesos but on the eve of my arrival at Veracruz it has been decreed that the series corresponding to my money did not have any value whatsoever. I then consulted with my friend Treasurer General Barragan who in a humorous manner took my bills and made an appointment for me to meet him at this same place the next day. And thus, it was that the next day I had in my possession new currency which was then in circulation. The constitutional forces, on their second attack, after having failed on the first one, entered Mexico City which was then being held by Zapatista forces.

Since the leaders were still at the Port of Veracruz, the various subordinate chiefs of the Secretariat of State started to organize the services in Mexico City. Mr.

Adolfo de la Huerta in the capacity of Senior Officer of the Secretariat of Government to which I was assigned directed me to organize and assign personnel to the House for Abandon Children named Casa de Cuna situated at the ancient Colegio de Macarones. After having completed this assignment in about a month, I was then assigned as Administrator and External Medical Officer of the General Hospital. In that medical medium I once again entered my professional activities at the side of some masters such as Dr. Rosendo Amor, Dr. Dario Fernandez, Dr. Manuel Castillejos, Dr. Cleophas Padilla, and others whom I no longer recall.

The activities in the administration of the general hospital are quite complicated; therefore, in order to tend to them the Administrator is assigned a magnificent residence together with all the pertinent services located within the hospital grounds. I lived there with all the conveniences for two years. I had as Director of the Establishment, Dr. Alfonso Cabrera, a very competent professional who was proficient in carrying out his duties. Upon completing my assignment as Administrator and External Medical Officer, I resigned and decided returned to my home state and my hometown.

"In his own hometown, no one is a prophet," says the old adage, which turned out to be quite true upon returning to my hometown. Even though I did not seek it I became involved in local politics, and I became a candidate for the post of local Deputy or Representative, taking

175

into account my revolutionary affiliations and the fact that I was the native-born professional from my hometown. With an overwhelming margin over my opponent Aurelianus Mijores, I won the election. Nonetheless, even though I thought I had all the necessary credentials already in my pocket and was now ready to accept my legislative seat, the cold relationship that existed between me and the Governor of the State Lic. Gustavo Espinoza Mireles caused my triumph to be changed to a loss by a very simple maneuver of which there are many in the field of politics.

Only for one purpose of explaining this maneuver do I describe it so that there will not remain any suspicion whatsoever. The Rules of the Chamber of Deputies established that in order to decree the triumph of a candidate the Deputies shall meet in session with the winners of the elections being present at such meeting on a prior determined date. It was very simple, for internal political reasons, this meeting was called, I was never notified and therefore I was not present, and the triumph was awarded to my opponent.

Two months prior to this most disagreeable incident the destinies of my life had changed. I united in matrimony with Miss Evangelina Avila, native of my hometown, San Pedro de las Colonias, daughter of Don Antonio B. Avila and his wife Sra. Aurelia Vargas de Avila. I had married and now lived happily at the side of my beautiful and adorable companion. With total satisfaction and sincerity, I must express that my happiness at the side of my wife, "Calina" who presented me with two fine offspring, my adorable daughter, Leticia and my unforgettable son Jose Mauro, may he rest in peace.

A year now having passed, once again, state politics became agitated and when I least expected it without having been consulted, I was named Municipal President or the Mayor of my hometown by the new Governor of the State, General Arnulfo Gonzalez. The State Legislature decreed my appointment. The environment this appointment placed me in as the primary authority in the town did not coincide with my own ideas. I could not conceive having in one hand the stethoscope to auscultate my patients and in the other hand the rod of justice, which had to be applied to my patients. Therefore, it was at this juncture that I elected to renounce the position of Municipal President and leave this hometown that darkened my way and absorbed me into politics, which to me is the worst road that a medical professional can follow.

On a vacation trip I took my family to San Antonio, Texas for a stay of one month. During the time I spent in this city, on the advice of a Dr. Paschal, Sr. who I had met through a recommendation of my friend Sr. Don Emilio Madero, the brother of President Madero, I submitted my application to obtain my medical license from the State of Texas to be able to practice my profession. One month later I received a reply from the Texas Board of Medical Examiners that my application was accepted and

177

consequently in one month I was to be in Austin, Texas, to take the corresponding examination. Now with my license from the State of Texas in my hands I returned not to my hometown but Sabinas, Coahuila, where I planned to establish my practice.

By a true coincidence and genuine happenstance, on the day I arrived in Sabina, at the same hotel where I was staying, there was registered Dr. Federico Margain, who enrolled with me in the National Medical School in Mexico City years earlier. Federico changed his option during our first year of medicine and enrolled in the Dental School, from which he later graduated. After having greeted each other effusively the important interrogation followed: "What are you doing here?" "I have come to here practice." "So am I." "Do you have a place already set aside?" "No." "Well neither do I." "No." "Well neither do I." "Shall we look for one where we can both install ourselves?" "Sure, we can." "Do you have your family with you?" "No." Well, neither do I." "I have a drug store." I said, "and I plan to bring it here but do not have anyone to take charge of it." I will take charge of it" he stated, "and we will split the expenses and utilities." We came to an understanding and started looking for a place for our families, and for the drug store.

The first year passed quite well but the following year bad luck came to me and my family. My good wife, Calina, who helped me so much, became seriously ill to such a degree that I felt it was best to take her to San Antonio,

Texas where her condition worsened to the point that a surgical intervention became necessary and with continuing bad luck, the third day after surgery, she passed away.

Now, being completely disoriented and saddened by the irreparable loss of my adorable companion I returned to Sabinas with all faith lost and my heart destroyed. I remained there accompanied by my two children for a few months until Frederico and I agreed to move to Piedras Negras, Coahuila. Frederico and his virtuous wife offered me their home to help with my children who were still very young and needed the warmth of a home. A few months after having been installed in Piedras Negras I received word that Dr. Meave was gravely ill. A few days later he would pass away, and this sad event once again changed the destinies of my life. Remembering that I had a license to practice medicine in Texas, Mrs. Meave, the widow of Dr. Meave, invited me to come live there where I could use her house as a home for my children. I accepted the invitation and went to live in San Antonio and work in the office Dr. Meave had left.

In this uncertain and tempestuous manner my life and my children's lives were slipping by. Not having any desire to return to my country, I was now forming many illusions, thinking about my solitude, and the abandonment my children were undergoing, in their need of a home and so many other things. Only my will power and inner fortitude helped me overcome my despair. In that house while we certainly did not lack anything. There was attention, courtesy, and care towards me and my children, nonetheless nothing could fill the emptiness left by loss of my wife. Accompanying Mrs. Meave were her nieces Catalina, Aurelia, and Chabela who were the joy of that house. Notwithstanding, there was a marked and noticeable attention and tenderness as well as self-denial in Catalina towards my children and towards me which at the moment started to give birth within me the idea that perhaps Catalina could fill the emptiness and return to us the happiness we were now lacking. I then commenced to distinguish and direct my attention to her, and at the same time there started to germinate the fondness which was transforming into love. She comprehended my feelings and little by little I began to see she was responding to my attention.

Not very much timed passed when, after thinking it over well, I proposed matrimony to her. After having thought it out cautiously and thinking about the great responsibility she would be undertaking she accepted my proposal which was a great pleasure to the both of us. Of course, we right away told Mrs. Meave so that she might make it known to the rest of the family. The news received the approbation of all our relatives and our relationship now became formalized.

Accommodating ourselves to our social position we planned our matrimony for the 30th of April 1925. It was a modest wedding, but a most attractive and a well-attended one. As Godparents we had Dr. and Mrs. Joaquin

Gonzalez Cigarroa Sr. and Dr. and Mrs. Federico Margain. We planned our wedding trip to Del Rio, Texas taking advantage at the same time of a proposition being made to me to come establish my practice in this city. Without offending the memory of my late first wife, Calina who made me happy and content, I give thanks to God for having placed along the way in my life Cata, who with res- ignation, self-denial and love accompanied me in forming a happy home with our four children—Yolanda, Simon Jr., Rosa Marta, and Rolando. In parting from these events, a new chapter in my life opens up which well deserves that I recall it because it covers a period of 31 years wherein there is no longer room for the restlessness of the youth- ful years, but now for the repose of a home life, which in summary, is the fulfillment of an obligation, the education of a family.

# The Magician

**B**ACK IN THE EARLY 70'S THERE WAS A TELEVISION SERIES called "The Magician" with Bill Bixby as the lead actor. The show ran one season with a total of twenty-one episodes. I have no idea how the creator of the show came up with the idea of a crime fighting magician who saves lives and solved complex crimes with magic. When "The Magician" aired, I watched every episode intensely, writing down the tricks Tony Blake, Bill Bixby's character, performed. I learned all his tricks. I talked with Tony while he performed on television, I was one of his biggest fans. He was my idol. He drove a Corvette and owned a private jet. The jet was his home. It was like a Winnebago with wings. The show was cancelled after one season. It was rated number 51 out of a possible 52 shows for the season. "Me and the Chimp" took last place in the ratings. I liked that show too. I like that show too. It was about a chimp that washed out of the NASA space program. Needless to say, I was devastated. I don't think my taste in television shows ever improved to this day. I always felt I could have been on that show.

I started practicing magic when I was three months old, or so my parents said. I recall my parents telling me time and time again that it was magical how a little blip of a human could produce such extremely pungent and plentiful gifts, so frequently. I was able to perform this feat without thinking about it. I was told crowds would gather in disbelief and stare down as I smiled with a gaseous ear to ear grin. It was always a short-lived performance, but nevertheless, my career as a magician was cast early in life.

My interest in magic became more center stage when I reached the age of six. I was involved in the grub scouts, and at one grub scout awards banquet I was chosen to be the assistant for a real magician. He did the old block through the blockhead trick. The illusion involved two empty but colorful rectangular boxes about twelve inches long, by about four inches square. The magician puts one block on top of the assistants' head and the another is held over the mouth. The magician then produces a mul-ticolored three-inch by three-inch square wooden block and passes it through the first rectangular tube, through the assistant's head and it then appears to fall out of the tube positioned over the mouth. The he does it again, and again. The patter, as I recall, inferred there was nothing in the way to prevent the solid block of wood from passing right through the assistant's head. Applause! Applause! Applause! Snickers from the audience suggested the master magician could not have chosen a better assistant for the trick. I was affectionately referred to as "Blockhead" by my family for years following that performance. Eventually I would have the affectionate nickname "Egghead". It had nothing to do with intelligence.

Soon after my stint as the assistant, I begged and pleaded with my beleaguered mom to take me to the library. The internet did not exist at that time and I needed books, real books. I wanted to learn about the art of magic. Upon finding the magic section in the stacks, I was engrossed for hours. I paged through book after book in awe. There before me was a world of secrets, deception and trickery. A new chapter in my short-lived life was opening up. I read about card tricks, sleight of hand, coin magic, bird magic, escape techniques, lock picking, secret invisible ink formulas, sponge ball routines, rabbit tricks and illustrious stage illusions like levitations and cutting people in half. What better way to win friends and influence people but through trickery and deception? Again, my lot in life was reaffirmed. I was going to be the worlds greatest magician, full of trickery and deception.

One of the first rules of being a successful magician is to never tell the secrets of magic tricks. I could not imagine why all the secrets were here for the taking. I figured some-one really messed up and left all the books on magic out in a public library for any common kid to find by mistake. I could not have that. I felt the urge to hide the secrets for the good of the Secret Society of Magicians. They were secrets after all. What self-respecting kid magician would intentionally break the first rule of being a real magician? I thought of a plan. First, I would steal all the books on magic. If I got caught and put in prison, big deal. I could escape. I had the book on escapology and knew the secrets. No stinking prison could hold me. I knew I could escape from straightjackets, handcuffs, cages, coffins, steel boxes, fish-tanks and burning buildings. I could hide all these secrets by burying them in my backyard. One by one, two by two, three by three, the books ended up in my room, under my bed. It only took twenty trips to the library.

It didn't happen the way I imagined. My plan for keeping magic secrets secret were dashed when my dad asked why I was digging a hole in the backyard. When I explained the problem, he carefully guided me back to his reality. I ended up filling in the hole and returning the snitched books, all eighty-five of them. Although I was not sent to prison, much to my dismay, I was confined to my room for a week. I soon realized there was no way to escape the confines of my room. That particular escape was not in the book. According to dad, the time in my room was to be spent reflecting on my wrongdoing. He made me write "I will not steal books from the public library" five hundred times while I was incarcerated. I thought my hand would fall off. I kept looking for a magic trick to do the task for me. He did not buy the argument that I was working on behalf of the Secret Society of Magicians and I was doing a service by stealing the books and keeping the secrets secret. I kept hoping I could cast a spell on my dad so he would see it my way. I would close my eyes really tight and mumble some Arabic sounding words like "ali banana, open sesame seeds, make my dad really believe me". It didn't work. It was the longest week of my young life, but not the end of it.

A few days after I was paroled from room confinement, I decided I needed to acquire doves to enhance my own magic show. I had no idea where I could find doves but knew I needed magical ones. Most magicians produced beautiful white doves. They performed glorious illusions with doves, and I knew I could do the trick, I had the secrets. Some doves were trained to perch on elaborate props waiting for the next miraculous feat. I realized I needed to add this to the next dimension of my magical repertoire. After some serious thought, I figured I could catch some mourning doves and train them. They were plentiful in our neck of the woods. I could hear the cooing, day in and day out. Because I was on a limited budget of zero funds, they would have to do. I took the initiative to build a dove trap. I found a rather large cardboard box, a stick and about half mile of braded nylon string. As I scrambled out of the house with the apparatus, I drifted through the kitchen and grabbed a loaf of Butterkrust sandwich bread to use as bait for the trap. I would also have a snack if the need arose. I set the trap up in a wooded park across the street from our house. It happened to be late in the afternoon and I knew I needed to be home for dinner. Thinking ahead, I set up the trap by propping the box up with the stick which had the string tied to it. Then I proceed to unwind the string across road until I was just about at the front door to our house. About that time, my dad came home from work and asked what I was up to. Nonchalantly, I responded "catching doves". He drifted back to his routine, not paying much attention to me. I soon realized I could not see the trap. I could not tell if the doves were actually going after the bait I carefully place in and around the trap. That was the first mistake. Just then, mom called us all to dinner. I decided to attach the string to the collar of Peppy, our cream-colored pet toy poodle, my reluctant magic show accomplice. That was my second mistake. I told him firmly, "Peppy Stay!" After a few minutes, mom asked if anyone had seen the new loaf of bread she just purchased for dinner. I looked her straight in the eye and said it must have disappeared. That was the third mistake. About that time, Peppy let out a horrendous cry. I immediately yelled "DOVES IN THE TRAP!" and bolted out the door looking for the string to pull to capture my magical doves. I saw Peppy being dragged by the string, barking and yelping. My mind was racing, thinking I must have caught a boatload of doves if they were pulling Peppy like that! Off I bolted towards the woods hoping to find my magical quarry, ignoring the plight of my faithful assistant. As I neared the trap, I could tell it worked! The box was in the fully closed position. I was so excited I wet my pants. I approached the box eager to lift the lid and inspect my magical doves. I could hear the trapped quarry flapping around and banging the inside of the box. Finally, I would have the magical doves to enhance my magical aspirations. I got down on my hands and knees and approached quietly. As I tilted the box to gaze in and marvel at the catch and I was greeted with a WHOOOSH spray of potent perfume right in the face. It was my first encounter with a live skunk. That blast sent me to the moon, coughing and spitting. Spinning around, through tear-filled eyes, I saw my parents chasing after Peppy. The nylon braided string attached to Pappy's collar was tangled in the axle of a passing 1965 Chevy Nova and dragged the two-pound hound effortlessly.

The driver of the Nova finally stopped when he heard my parents yelling at the top of their lungs. My parents were able to rescue Peppy, all of them shaking with fear. As I made my way home with the empty box, a broken stick, a half mile of tangled cord, wet britches and choking on skunk spray, fear enveloped me. I knew I was in trouble, and it was going to get worse. It was the first night I spent camping outside alone. Even Peppy avoided me for several days. After the twentieth bath, I was incarcerated to my room for another week. This time, I had to write "I will not lie to mom, ever" and "I will not steal bread." and "I will not tie Peppy to traps." Five hundred times each. It was turning out to be a lousy summer.

That fall on the first day of school, I met Jamie Grant. He was another aspiring magician. He didn't have doves, he had chickens. Magical Chickens. That was the beginning of the end to my magical career.

# The Pioneers

T HIS IS ABOUT KEEPING A PROMISE...

It was back in the mid-1800's. Many families, looking for new opportunities left their roots in Europe to search for a better life in the new country. For many the country was America, a land of abundance, freedom of political and religious expression, taxation with representation, chance for families to grow and prosper. Such it was for the Donner family. They immigrated to the west coast with the dream of going into the cattle business in California. In the spring of 1844, George Donner was positioning his family to migrate west to California. The journey would take 4-6 months, figuring the ox drawn wagons would make 3-4 miles a day at best. It was imperative to get thru the mountain passes before the winter snows started. The trail west was treacherous. They heard this from the mountain men and Native Americans that acted as guides for anxious pioneers. About 35-50 percent of the people that started the trip would not make it. Some of the pioneers got lost; many others would die from disease such as consumption, many newborns died during childbirth and the mothers would soon follow.

The Donner family was part of a larger wagon train that had made it thru the Wasatch Mountains to Salt Lake City. That was a major resupply stop for many of the travelers. At this stop, they would buy and sell livestock, repair the wagons and get nursed back to health. It was late September, and the leader of the Donner party knew the snow would be coming soon. The larger wagon train split up and some of the travelers already left. There were two routes to consider taking. One was the more commonly traversed northern route. It was longer but it was less strenuous. It was preferred route for many. The southern route was over some significant mountain passes with elevations reaching ten thousand feet plus. But, if you could make it thru the passes on this route, you would cut about two hundred miles off the trek.

The Donners and several other families in the party were getting a late start. They needed to make up time. After the group had discussed the options, they chose to take the faster southern route. They would be traveling early October and the elk would be in rut. They felt there would be ample fresh meat. The odds looked pretty good as the weather was mild. As they started towards the northern California Mountains, they notice smatterings of snow in the highest peaks. The trail up to the passes was steep and arduous. The ox and horses were starting to show early signs of exhaustion and grasses were less available, the trail was difficult. Several oxen were slaughtered for food early on, as the wild game was not as abundant as expected. This worried George Donner.

They reached a high mountain pass in the high Sierra Nevada and setup camp on the edge of Truckee Lake in mid-November. The temperature at night would drop well below freezing. The night they set up camp it started to snow, and it kept snowing for the next week. The weather had turned bad and it was freezing not only at night, but also during the day. Their clothing, although the best they could afford, was worn and tattered. Some of the weaker travelers became sick. They were able to inhabit two crudely constructed cabins built two years earlier. The snow kept falling. Within a few short days over 18 feet of snow had fallen and it kept coming. The Donner party was stuck. They could not go back, and they could not move forward. The after about two weeks, sick started to die and then some of the youngest. Some people froze to death. As the horses died, they would butcher and eat what they could. They could not hunt. They started to develop scurvy, as they had no fruits or vegetables. Food went from scarce to non-existent, and starvation raised its sickly grip in the beleaguered bodies of the remaining party members. They became desperate eating tree bark, and the leather from the ox and then the horses. In the end the surviving members of the party reverted to cannibalism and started to eat the dead.

Of the original 85 members of the Donner party, 43 were alive at the time the first rescue team from California arrived. The first rescue party reached the stranded travelers four months after getting stuck. Historians have described the episode as one of the most bizarre and harrowing tragedies in Californian history and western-US migration.

This is where the story takes a turn and I needed to keep a promise.

I met Mr. Jim Hazard about 15 years ago. He was the Charter Organization Representative to our Boy Scout Troop. Jim passed away in March 2010. He was an Eagle Scout and had done much of his scouting in California. He told me some great stories about scout camps he attended. He was in the Order of the Arrow, gone on numerous fifty-mile backpacking trips, was a Scoutmaster, Unit Commissioner and received the prestigious Silver Beaver award many years ago. He was a true and trusted scout his whole life. Before he passed away, at age of 77, he asked me to come by.

During our conversation, he relayed his story of the Donner party. As he was talking, he reached into his desk drawer and pulled out an old small leather bag. Inside was a small metal brand. He told me that some of the surviving Donner party, the Reed family, had gone into cattle ranching in California and that this was their brand. Over the years he became friends with members of the family. He was in Boy Scouts with some of the great-great-great grandkids of the original Donner party. The family recognized Jim's passion for scouting and his pioneering spirit. The family presented Jim with this brand with the instructions to please pass the story on.

Before Jim died, during my meeting with him, he asked me to keep the story alive. He asked me to look for opportunities to share the history of the Donner Party, a true story of survival, of pioneers that were not fortunate, but symbolized the spirit of adventure, the outdoors and survival. Jim told me this is the only such brand in existence and that it was given to him to share with the scouts. It you ever see someone with it; they probably know the story about the Donner Party.

As I was preparing for summer camp, I started to think about an opportunity to share this story and honor the promise I made to Jim. I branded a small leather piece for each of the staff members at Camp Pioneer. I presented one to each of the staff members for making Camp Pioneer an exceptional opportunity for our youth to explore and savor. I believe this is in harmony with what the brand owners intended. The brand is a piece of our American history. This is a physical and tangible link with our past.

Thank you to the camp staff for providing the pioneering experience to the scouts. I salute you for providing your most valuable gift, your time, to our youth. I also thank you for allowing me the opportunity to fulfill a promise and pass a little of our American history to our scouts.

# The Story of Agnes

ER NAME WAS AGNES. "WHEN DID I FIRST MEET YOU?" I thought. "When did our paths first cross? Why did they cross?" I kept wondering if there was a reason for the enconter. Her hair was dirty blonde with a golden hue in the sunlight. She was tan and had a strong, firm, well-defined leg, ample breasts, and naturally pink lips. Her eyes were exceptionally captivating, piercing amber in colored. I was on the western coast of Spain. I sat at a small table in a quaint café nestled in the village of Finisterra. I was thinking about all the different people I encountered on the trail. I met Agnes early in the journey, near the city of Burgos. She was German, from Dusseldorf.

Pilgrims are easy companions. You see one and say hello and a conversation is started. Then moving along the Camino de Santiago, you travel to other places and meet other people. Sometimes your paths cross. I crossed paths with Agnes several times. We always engaged in frank discussions. We talked about food, relationships, politics, religion, blisters, children, and the weather. She was easy to talk to, and her smile and laugh comprised an utterly gripping, at least to me. She hated Donald Trump and thought he was an animal. She thought he was dangerous from a political standpoint and did not have any respect for women. She kept saying how he was explosive and unpredictable. I agreed with her for the most part.

As I was leaving the doctor's examination room at the alburgue in Puente La Reina I looked up through the opened door and I spied Agnes for the first time. She was checking in getting her bunk assignment. We looked at each other in a locked gaze. Her enticing amber eyes caught my attention. I nodded, and she smiled in acknowledgement. She was wearing non-descript light gray hiking shorts, a multi-colored scarf wrapped loosely around her head, a white simple V-neck t-shirt, voguish, simple, and elegant. Her red backpack looked worn but not shabby. When she smiled at me, I noticed a string of blondish hair pushing out of her scarf; her cheeks were tinged red and flushed from the heat of the day. She looked hot and thirsty. Her skin was flawless and tight. She was about 5'8" in height, tanned with long strong legs and a naturally tapered waist. She was a truly beautiful woman and the image of that first glance still lingers in my mind. But what would learn is that her beauty originated from deep within her soul.

I did not speak with her until the next morning as I limped out of the alburgue on another cool and cloudless morning. She and I happened to be leaving at the same time and she spoke in German telling me she understood why I was walking so gently, saying she was also concerned about blisters, but she felt well prepared and so far, not developed any issues with her feet. She was patient with my pace as I struggled to quell the agony, wanting to keep up with her, and yet not letting on that in every step I was experiencing excruciating pain. My German was rusty, but we managed to converse and eventually she started to speak in English.

Meeting up with Agnes was always engaging. Over the course of the Camino, we would randomly meet numerous times walking both in conversation and in silence. I noticed things about her that struck me as curious and delightful. She wore very little make-up yet exuded simple elegance, an air of refinement, sophistication and grace. As I had mentioned previously, the Europeans are much less inhibited than others and disrobe or change clothes with little or no thought of being watched. On two different occasions when we happened to be in the same alburgue, she would emerge from her bed and start a yoga or stretching routine in her under clothes or what little she slept in. I could not help myself but did avert my gaze as I could. It's difficult when a beautiful young woman, confident in herself is so scantily dressed.

I was starting to feel an upwelling of attraction slowly wondering and speculating on "what if's". I was asking myself if Agnes found me interesting and what if this was on a track to something more. I was feeling a stir of emotions that was supposed to be forbidden to me. I quickly snapped back to reality and thought that this was absurd to wonder about anything more than a platonic relationship with this young lady. Back in Oregon was a wonderful woman that I had made a promise to and although our 20 plus-year relationship had seen many bumps and trials of will, I was not going to jeopardize it. The temptation was great but I was not going to pursue Agnes or any other woman. That's not why I was here. I was on a spiritual pilgrimage, and I reflected that Agnes was a temptation. Our age difference was over 30 years. I could have easily been her father and perhaps that was why our paths had crossed. I do not claim to be wise and or anything that would hint that I know better than the next person. The only thing I could do was listen quietly, patiently and enjoy the company of a beautiful woman. Perhaps I would offer her advice based on the many mistakes I have made, that would be the best I could do and that would be all I would do. But that's not what happened.

It is interesting how easily pilgrims will discuss any variety of topics and so it was with Agnes. I recall an early morning meeting. It was a clear and cool and I had already stopped for a café con leche and a croissant. I was on the trail deep in personal thought battling philosophical questions of life. I could hear footsteps from behind and then I heard her say in a guttural yet dulcet German voice "Gutten Morgen". It was her voice and delicate smile with slightly pursed red lips and amber colored eyes that captivated me. As we walked, we talked about our lives and Agnes told me about her job and that she was working with troubled youth from ages 7 to 18. She enjoyed the work especially the ability to develop trust and make a connection with young people who had had a difficult young life. Many were from broken families and abused sexually or emotionally or both. Her job, she explained, was to develop trust becoming a friend, mentor, counselor and confidant. She had attended university in Hannover and was completing her studies working as an intern outside of school. Her field of study was psychology, specifically the adolescent years. At one point in our conversations Agnes became somewhat contemplative and told me she was working as a camp counselor in Norway when the worst mass killing in that country occurred. This happened in summer of 2011 and I remembered the story about 77 teens that were shot by a deranged man at a youth retreat. Agnes was there as an intern when it occurred and she still had horrible memories and bad dreams about the event. Her camp mentor was killed. She went on explaining how it was a miracle she wasn't killed and that she was not in the building where the shooting attack occurred but felt she would have been in a few minutes. She had left to retrieve a Bible she left in her room just prior to the attack. Apparently, the man had set off several small bombs and then went on a shooting rampage in a large room where the young students had gathered. She did come to help the victims. In doing so she witnessed the carnage of the death and the trauma of wounded people. She said it was the most horrifying thing she had ever seen and re-affirmed her commitment to help troubled youth wherever she could. She felt if she could help prevent this kind of tragedy from happening, she would be content with her life. Agnes was very emotional during this conversation and I could tell it still troubled her deeply.

We walked in silent for a long while. Then I asked if she had ever owned a gun and she laughed. She explained she owned many weapons that belonged to her father. He passed away about 10 years ago and she had inherited a fine collection of firearms including pistols, military weapons, shotguns, large caliber hunting rifles and ancient medieval torture devices. She was an only child when he passed away and she went on to tell me about her first hunt. It was with her father about 25 years ago. He took her to hunt stags in the Blackforest just north of Munich. She remembered they traveled to a hunting chalet deep in the dark recesses of the mountainous region of the Blackforest, arriving well after dark. Upon entering a dimly lit grand hall, she was awe-struck by the ominous shadows of the mounted heads of great stags that had been harvested from the area in years passed. The deer were huge. At the young age of five, Agnes was captivated. A roaring fire was in a massive stone fireplace and fellow hunters surrounded a long heavy wooden table, drinking beer from large multi-colored steins. They were the Burgermeisters or forest masters of the surrounding lands and were employed by an Obermeister or overseer and a Baron employed the Obermeister. Agnes's father and grandfather and great-great grandfather and many generations back were land Barons of huge hunting reserves throughout the Blackforest region. They were land barons of Germany entrusted generations ago with the stewardship and responsibility of caring for and maintaining the forest resources and that included the wild game. Agnes was a baroness, a woman of nobility and a huntress and she was sexy.

In pre-republic Germany all knightly families of the Holy Roman Empire were recognized as baronial rank and persons that held that rank enjoyed a distinction of nobility or as I interpreted it, a noble. No wonder Agnes carried herself in such a polished and refined fashion. She was European nobility. As we talked she went on to say that she did not have a boyfriend. She had had several suitors over the last several years, as she really did not start dating until she was 20 years old. Agnes told me her mother pretty much left her alone and that she had a trust fund and inheritance that she could live on. Her mother lived in Vienna and drank heavily after her father passed. She and her mother drifted apart. Agnes also told me that her family also held title to several houses, chalets, and apartments in various parts of Germany and in several cities throughout Europe. She really did not have to work but she had a passion for what she was doing. It did not pay much but that really did not matter. She was able to live off what she made and she never let on that she was of aristocracy. She had traveled pretty much wherever and whenever she wanted and was fluent in German, French, Spanish and English and had studied Latin. She played the cello for the orchestra in Hannover, the NDR Radiophilharmonie, and seemed to be proud of this. The NDR Radiophilharmonie, she explained, is a radio orchestra affiliated with the Nord-Deutscher Rundfunk (NDR) and gives concerts in the Grossberg Sendesaal a state broadcasting station in Hannover the capital of Lower Saxony. She went on to say the broadcast could be heard around the world and that I should tune into it when I returned home.

Agnes went saying she had been thinking about one of her suitors while walking and started telling me about him. He was a Frenchman and came from a family with title. In order to keep the rank of baroness, Agnes explained she would need to marry a fellow aristocrat or relinquish the title. Their families had known of each other for many years as they attended several functions together such as coronations, weddings, and subsequent receptions. Dante, the Frenchman, had a slight build and was a sickly-looking young boy as Agnes recalled and he really didn't have an adventurous spirit. He was bright and a good fencer but did not have an interest in exploring and traveling. His passion was oil painting and she had posed for him nude once and was not happy with the final picture. She said he walked like Charlie Chaplin with more of a waddle than a walk and that she felt kind of sorry for him. She would not marry him, but said she found him kind and generous. Agnes explained that she was walking the Camino because her father had done so many years ago. She said she also hoped to find more meaning in her spiritual life, and she was seeking out some of the simple places her father had written about in his journals.

Once Agnes had brought up her father's journals, she asked me what I knew about WWII. I told her I had an interest but that I was not a scholar in the subject, but my father had served in the Pacific Theater, and he had a brother named Mauro, who was lost at sea when his B-29 bomber was shot down. She went on to talk about some of the stories her father documented in his journals. One story involved a 13th century monastery located in the foothills of the Thuringian Forest near the Bavarian mountains. Agnes said that deep in the forest referenced in the journals was a cave near the area she hunted as a youth. She recalled going to the area with her father many years ago. He told her this was a secret place and where several projects had gone on here during the war. She said she remembered the chambers they had entered had crates upon crates stacked to a high ceiling. The monks at the monastery built a series of tunnels over the generations. The tunnels came up at a certain unmarked locations and it was said that they would bring wine to the locations and the local villagers would bring goods to trade. She remarked that she had been wondering if the treasures were still secreted away.

As we entered the small village of Lorca, I told Agnes I needed to find a restroom. She said she did as well. That would mean we would likely have to stop and purchase something from the shopkeeper or that was what I assumed was customary. I learned it was not expected and that many shopkeepers along the Camino understood the need and they would rather you use their facility than go outside and dirty up the place. I told Agnes that I would meet her down the trail in a while. Our paths would not cross for the next week.

Agnes was a latecomer to the young group of shade seekers. She easily slipped in and out of the group with ninja like stealth. When she disappeared, she was missed, and the group would ask where she had gone. When she re-appeared, laughter would erupt, and comments flew about her absents. She offered up quick wit and motivating enthusiasm that focused the clutch of friends. In my opinion, Agnes was unique and her passion for life was infectious. Her simple elegance and generous nature made her an unyielding inspiration for the small community of acquaintances. She became fast friends with the group. I asked her why she was walking the Camino. She explained with her strong Germanic accent that it was an unexplainable pull from her past. She went on to say it was a desire to walk and seek truth in the simplicity of life. She was religious but had not practiced faithfully in many years. She said she was an Easter, Christmas Catholic. She also felt that the Camino was impacting her faith, but she could not explain how just yet. I was consistently dazzled by her engaging smile, charming wit, striking beauty and passionate conversation.

The next morning, I headed out early. I had slept well and felt rested and had new energy. Agnes joined me early in the morning and we walked together for a longtime.

I think about Agnes every now and then. I wonder how she is doing. She will always soar above the clang and the clatter of life in my memory.

# The Thinking Chair

I S FURNITURE UNDERRATED? I DON'T KNOW THE ANSWER TO
this question, but I do know that we learn to live inti-
mately with the items we acquire over our lives to
furnish our homes. We purchase tables of all kinds, dinner
tables, kitchen tables, computer tables, end tables, coffee
tables, sewing tables and the like. We acquire bookshelves,
both tall and short, desks, cabinetry, and chairs. What is
perplexing to me, is how we have grown attached to these
inanimate objects in an almost sub-conscience and mostly
sentimental ways. They become our friends, our favor-
ites, the best and mine. They become part of our family in
peculiar ways. Are we attached to certain items or are they
attached to us? We struggle with furniture and tote items
with us, sometimes all over the world. We have probably inherited some pieces of furniture from our parents,

or a family member and that item will have developed an emotional or sentimental thread of love for the owner embedded in the fabric or leather or wood.

One item of furniture I recently sold has brought an upwelling of emotional sentiment for me. We affectionately called it "the thinking chair". It was given this name by my wife when my older son Simon was about three years of age. "Blue's Clues" a cartoon show on Public Broad Service channel, had a large (cartoon) overstuffed red chair which offered a retreat for the characters to sit in and ponder the "clues", missing pieces of a puzzle. My son and I would sit together and think about the clues. He would climb up on my lap and in a curious way show me his thinking face. I would tell him to think harder, and he would strain with his closed eyes even more tightly and with such conviction, I thought his head might explode if he kept it up.

My wife and I bought the chair off a furniture store show room floor in Richland, Washington, 20 plus years ago. It was one of the first pieces of furniture we bought as a married couple, about a year before our first son arrived. It was an overstuffed light colored leather recliner. It was comfortable with stitching on the arms and penny sized brass brad tacking along the edges. As you pushed against the arms, a footrest would rise from the bottom front, providing a hidden cavity underneath the seat. It was just the right size for a small child to hide in. I tended to use the chair in the afternoons when I would return from work. I would read the paper or open the mail or watch the evening news in the comfort of the well-made chair.

When our first son arrived, I would hold him in my arms and on my chest and we would nap together in the chair. Mostly I would marvel at this small incredible creation I had been blessed with, watching with intense joy as each small breath would draw in and back out. We would spend a lot of time in that chair. About 20 months later my second son Mateo would arrive. Again, I would have the joy of his infancy and cradling him to sleep on my chest, in the thinking chair. The chair retained several stains from uncleaned burping events, the odors being long gone. As the boys grew, the chair would record certain events in its folds of leather. The scratch marks of young fingernails could be seen. Neither of the boys would admit to putting them there, but it did not really matter. The black pen marks soon faded with time, and I have a hard time remembering which child had the creative spurt to write on the leather. Truth be told, it really did not matter. We would watch the boys use the chair as part of the forts they would build, covering it with blankets and sheets and pillows to conceal their whereabouts from an invisible enemy. The removable cushion would be their first trampoline. The chair would always figure prominently in a game of hide and seek; under the footrest was the best place. As they grew, I would witness their ferocious yet innocent battles to be first in the chair, and end up sharing the comfort of the supple leather armchair together.

My wife and I would occasionally share the chair together, she in my lap, holding each other tightly and comfortably. She would also find it a relaxing refuge as the tasks of being a mother and wife would find her exhausted at the end of a long day. If one of the boys were ill, they looked for comfort by curling up in the chair with a blanket and pillow and slept. As the boys grew, so would the marks of our life on the chair. The stains of tears would come and fade, as they would find comfort and solace in the broad soft arms of the aging leather. I forget which of the boys danced in the chair with muddy shoes, but it really did not matter. The mud was easily cleaned up. Our pet cats, Cappy and Tassu left their markings until we trained them to know the chair was not a scratching post.

It was also known as "Dad's chair" but it was used by all of us. The arms of the chair grew browner with age and use, so did the footrest. As the leather became darker, the back started to show stains from sweaty backs, as we would seek comfort from summertime activities, like yard work or games. Sometimes it would be race to the chair first or calling "Save for me!" identifying the chair was saved for use by that family member. When the boys were young, I would read from some favorite books as we gathered on the chair. Christmas eve, Carole would read typical stories such as "'Twas the Night before Christmas" and "The Christmas Package" with the young boys listening intently to the magical stories. A few years back, I found a broken spring under the chair as I vacuumed the floor. As I inspected the chair, I noted that several brass tacks were missing. The arms of the chair were cracking, and the back was showing signs of age, with worn bare spots from hitting the walls. When I removed the cushion, the Velcro was matted with old hair, small pieces of tape and paper, the general detritus from years of use.

A few weeks ago, I found myself in a furniture store. I had no intension of replacing the thinking chair. I spotted a new chair with a much more streamline appearance. When I sat in it, I felt a spark of guilt. It was comfortable and it swiveled. The thinking chair did not swivel, and it was looking old and worn. On impulse, I made the purchase. I brought the new chair home and with no discussion with the family, and I took the thinking chair to a consignment shop. The shop manager asked me how much he should ask for the chair and I stopped to think about the thinking chair. How could I put a price on the history of that old family friend? It had been well used and well loved. Although it had many scars from use, I realized it was time to say goodbye. I told him two hundred dollars.

The store manager called me saying the chair sold within an hour to a nice older lady. She had commented that it was just right. I am sure she will enjoy the comfort of that old friend and I wished I could tell her of the many hours of comfort that chair brought.

When Simon came home that afternoon from school the first thing he noticed and asked about was the chair. Where was it? What had happened? Was the family breaking apart? Are we moving? He was truly upset almost to the point of tears. I started to wonder if I had made a mistake. It's funny how we grow attached to things, like chairs. After thinking about the thinking chair for a long while, I think the answer to the question is that we underrate our furniture. It grows in value to those that find value and attachment in it. That's all I have to say about that.

# The Three-Legged Chicken

## A Tribute to President Reagan

This is a true story. Yesterday, my son Andrew approached me, looking a little priggish. I'm always quite concerned when he looks this way. I think he is sharp otherwise, (but I'm his dad). He started to explain that his current class load was fun, but relatively difficult. His part-time job with the genetic engineering company in Cambridge often kept him late into the evenings.

Mentioning his recent encounter with one senior researcher left him feeling somewhat concerned, Andrew told me he had been invited to dinner at his colleague's house.

The following day while making his way down a country lane north of Boston to the house, Andrew glanced in his rearview mirror and saw a white chicken running up behind his Zip car. Eyeing the odometer, he saw he was doing well over thirty-five miles per hour. When he looked up again, the chicken was running right alongside him and passing the car. Andrew shook his head and looked again. It appeared the chicken was running on three legs. Blinking a few times and seeing the chicken turn into a driveway just ahead of him, he followed it. The driveway happened to belong to his colleague. A bit down the drive he spotted his friend standing in the yard.

Andrew immediately asked him, "Did you see a chicken run past here?"

"Yep."

"Did it look like he had three legs?"

"Yes, I engineer them that way." He said.

Andrew thought about this for a minute and asked, "Why?"

The researcher replied, "You see I am kind of partial to the drumsticks, as is my wife. And well, when my son came along, he also took a liking to drumsticks. And so, in order to not squabble, I modified my chickens to grow three legs."

Andrew was a bit mystified and asked "Well, how do they taste?"

To which the collogue responded, "I don't know. I haven't been able to catch one."

Andrew thought about it for a while, and said, "Well, if you grow those chickens with three wings, they'll fly around in circles, and be easier to catch."

Three months later, my son was invited to dinner again. It was quite good dinner with an abundance of drumsticks and chicken wings.

# What We Take with Us

I MET CAROLYN RODGERS IN 2006 WHEN MY SON TURNED SIX years old. He was attending Garfield elementary school as a first grader. She was with her husband Jim. As the story goes, there was a cub scout recruitment sign on the corner of Garfield and Dixon which indicated a meeting was being held on Tuesday evening, 6:30 at Calvin Presbyterian church. I was a cub scout and I remember having a good time. I recalled fun adventures with the scouts during that period of my young life. I wanted my boys to have similar experiences. My mom was a den leader and Carolyn reminded me of her, especially when she was in her leaders' uniform.

We decided to attend the meeting the following week. When we arrived, I introduced my family and told Carolyn and Jim I wanted to help. The next thing I remember is Carolyn and Jim extending their hands and to shake mine vigorously saying, "Welcome aboard, Cubmaster!" I almost felt snookered into the program, but I knew I wasn't. The Rodgers were offering me and my family a beautiful opportunity. From then on, I would see Carolyn and Jim time and time again. They attended Roundtable meetings, Pow Wow events in Eugene, Camp Baker Scout Camp, the local Scout -O-Rama meeting, and frequent cub scout meetings. The interesting thing was they were always together. I was never sure if she was with Jim or the other way around.

I never learned a lot about Carolyn's youth. I understand she was a girl scout in her formative years, and she attained the Gold Star Scout Award, the highest level of recognition in the program. She was a den leader and a Woodbadge trainer. Woodbadge is the highest level of adult leader training the Boy Scouts of America offers. The program uses the "patrol method" of leadership and the patrols are designated by animals as their totem. Carolyn was an "Owl". Once the training is completed, the individual remains a part of that patrol for life. It is a brother/sisterhood in the Woodbadge Program. I am an Antelope and whenever we are in a meeting, and a participant completes their ticket, we sing the "Back to Gilwel". A customary song of comradery. All the individual critters group together. We had that in common and I believe she enjoyed singing as much as I did. She was proud to be an owl. One thing I know about Carolyn is that she helped a lot of people, including me. It was her nature to help others and treat people with kindness. She was a good person.

Carolyn was interesting in several ways. I recall one cub scout Blue and Gold Awards Banquet when she arrived with a "Tater-Tot Casserole". It was the first time I ever seen one. It was baked in a Pyrex dish, the tots were golden brown and covered with rich, stringy cheddar cheese. I don't think it was healthy, but it tasted good, and the cubs devoured it in a matter of minutes. I learned Carolyn, while raising her children was also employed as a high school home economics teacher.

Despite busy schedules, we always managed to keep in touch. A few years ago, Carolyn called and asked if she and Jim could be of assistance with Scout Troop 170. I had recently taken on the position of Scout Master for the troop. She explained that they moved to a new house near the meeting place and driving any distance at night was becoming more challenging for Jim. She felt they could make it to the meeting without too much difficultly. I told her I could use a citizenship merit badge counselor for the scouts. Citizenship in the Community, Citizenship in the Nation and Citizenship in the World merit badges are required to achieve the rank of Eagle. Carolyn and Jim jumped right in. They would come on Monday nights and counsel boys through the merit badges with great patience.

They enjoyed the interactions and working with the scouts, even though it could be challenging at times.

In some Native American Indian tribes, the elders have the honor to walk backwards during Ceremonial Pow Wow events. One tribe I visited in the past were the Kamloops band of the Shuswap Nation in western Canada. They are a proud people with many strong beliefs. They believe by walking to the left instead of the right, during a Pow Wow ceremony, they honor and share in the memories and spirits of their ancestors. They recall memories of their parents, grandparents, brothers, sisters, friends, enemies, and children they have lost. Walking in the circle in a reverse direction for all others, they acknowledge the spirits from the past and give thanks to their spirits. It is a form a prayer. A campfire going in the center of the circle and the fire symbolizes the core spirit of mankind.

On a recent bike ride on New Year's Eve, my wife and I peddled our usual route backwards. It was a good ride and provided me time to think. It was cool and gray, and soft. It felt like more rain was coming. The puffy clouds looked like dirty cotton balls. I was thinking a lot about Carolyn. I was thinking about her scouting spirit, and why spirit is important to family and friends. As I get older, I have learned that life will probably end sooner than we want it to. While we are blessed with each day, there seem to be so many details that consume our time and derail us from what is important. I wondered. Then I came up with what I think might be part of the answer, part of the mystery I have been searching for and why I will miss Carolyn so much. It's part of us that remains when we die. It is the spirit you leave behind. Carolyn, I appreciate and love your spirit.

When I think of Carolyn's spirit, I see and feel a bright campfire. I see the bright campfire of her life. Her spirit was calm but strong and warm. She shared her spiritual strength with family and community. It was a commitment to build a better world. The scouting spirit will remain strong because of her passion. She "passed it on" so to say. She ignited a spark in so many to follow simple values and to live full and helpful and lives worth living. They may not realize this, but they will always be grateful, and someone will pass it on because of her. Thank you, Carolyn, for sharing your most valuable time and spirit with so many in such a positive and meaningful way. I want to end this homage to Carolyn with a passage I came across during my scouting career.

## A Scout's Prayer

(From Scouting in New South Wales)

We have hiked along life's pathway,
Our packs upon our backs,

We have pitched our tents and rested
Here and there along the tracks.
We have used our compass wisely
To guide us on our way
And hope to reach the campsite
Of our Great Chief Scout someday.

We have tried to be trustworthy -
Kept our honor high and clean,
We have been as loyal as any
To our Country and our Queen.
We have done our best at all times -
Kept our Promise—been prepared,
And hope our good deeds please Him
When at last our souls are bared.

We have lightened others' burdens,
With our smiles along the way,
We have kept our hand in God's hand,
Walked beside Him day by day.
And when our span of life runs out,
We'll make this gentle plea -
May we sit around His Campfire
At the Final Jamboree.

-- Thanks to Michael F. Bowman, DDC-Training, GW
Dist. Nat Capital Area Council

# When I Was a Kid

WEN I WAS TWELVE YEARS OF AGE, WE LIVED IN SAN Antonio. This area of Texas can be brutally hot and extremely humid during the summer. At that time, my older brother Antonio developed an interest in motorcycles and had purchased a red Suzuki 125cc street and trail bike. He would ride it to school and a part time job he had at H.E.B., a grocery store chain. Frequently, he would take the bike out to open fields behind our house and race around dirt trails that twisted throughout the grasslands like a bowl of spaghetti. Antonio also developed an interest in engines and would take pieces off his motorcycle clean them in gas, figure out how the item worked, and then re-install it on the cycle.

We lived in a middle-class subdivision called Camelot and we had neighbors all around us. I recall on one occasion, in early spring I brought home a stray kitten. I named the calico feline Patches, and I grew very attached to her over the summer. She was easily house broken and tended to prefer the garage where there was a cool concrete floor to lie on. It was also where we kept her food and litter box. My mother tolerated the cat, muttering that Patches should earn her keep by at least catching mice or cockroaches; no freebies or handouts in our house. Everyone earned their keep by doing chores or paying rent. My brother, two sisters and I did a lot of chores.

I recall that Patches would follow my mom around because she was the one that would feed her on a regular basis. Due to the challenge of feeding our family, six in total, my parents purchased a used upright deep freezer from a neighbor in the military who had orders and moving out of the area. He didn't want to take it with him. My mom and dad thought the freezer was a good idea for extra foods and just in case he got a deer during hunting season. The freezer had several tempered glass shelves and a large white wire basket type storage space on the bottom section. I think they paid $25.00 for it. My parents also rationalized that it was more economical to be able to buy certain food items in quantity, break them apart and freeze them for later use. They also felt good about helping a neighbor that needed to off-load the appliance. There was space in the garage for the deep freezer right near the door to the kitchen. We quickly learned the freezer iced up easily and required de-frosting on almost a monthly basis. This was partly due to the heat and humidity that settled in over the long Texas summers.

One exceptionally hot summer Saturday morning my mother decided it was a good time to defrost the freezer. The typical routine was that everything came out of the freezer and placed in two large red Coleman ice chests we used for long trips and camping. My brother and I would break off chunks of the frost from the freezer and eat them. My mother scolded us saying that ice was not good to eat. But we snuck chunks of ice and frost into our mouths anyway because it was cool and refreshing. My mother started the de-frost routine mid-morning, and it was already getting warm outside.

About noon, I noticed that Patches was not around. I was playing pinball on a machine my dad received as a rent payment from our rental house and my brother was working on a part to his motorcycle. Patches was around in the morning, but I could not find her in her usual cool resting spots in the garage. I asked my mom if she had seen the cat and she said "no". I ran upstairs and looked in my room and then each room in the entire house calling her name and rattling the container we kept her dry food in. I started to get a bit worried and asked my mom if she could help me find Patches. We searched the house, and soon my brother and sisters joined the hunt.

After about 30 minutes of unsuccessful searching, we met at the kitchen table to talk. This was getting serious. How could the cat up and vanish? Could Patches have been hit out front? The cat never wandered off because there were too many other bigger strays in the area. My mom said the last time she recalled seeing Patches was in the garage earlier in the morning. We all headed back out to the garage to search again in earnest for our lost pet. On a whim, I opened the door to the deep freezer and there in the wire basket, curled up in a tight ball, was Patches. She was shivering and small icicles hung off her whiskers. Her eyes were glazed over, and she could barely exert and audible "meow". Apparently, she slipped into the freezer un-noticed while my mother cleaned out the last of the frost. The unit was plugged in, and the quick freeze cycle was humming along. It was running for about two hours.

Everyone panicked. My sisters screamed. My mother had a dishtowel and quickly wrapped Patches in it, rubbing her vigorously. The cat was almost frozen solid. As my mother worked to try and thaw Patches out by rubbing her in the towel, she dropped Patches on to the concrete floor. Patches hit with a dull thud. My brother grabbed the cat and ran over to his motorcycle work area. He quickly picked up the jar containing the gas he used to clean parts of his motorcycle engine and a small plastic yellow funnel. We watched in questioning disbelief as he proceeded to force the funnel down the cat's mouth and poured in about two tablespoons of gasoline in.

After about 5 seconds, Patches ears set back. She started to growl in a deep raspy wave of a hum, stood up and shook all over. The hair on her back stood straight up and she bolted out of my brother's arms leaving a bloody pair of scratches behind on his long thin forearms. She spun around the garage five or six times, up the shelving on walls, knocking over random bottles of spray paint cans, jumping into the rafters, bouncing from one side to the other, all the time growling and hissing fiercely like a wild lion. She jumped down to the top of the freezer then back up into the rafters. She ran from one side of the garage to the other, spinning and contorting with her fur standing straight up. After about 5 minutes, Patches bolted down to the center of the garage floor, stopped, shook vigorously, and flopped over on her side. She lay motionless.

We were all in shock. My mom quickly turned to tend to my brother's scratch wounds as we looked at each other in disbelief. It was a day we would never forget. My dad was in his study and came out to see what all the ruckus was. He just shook his head and headed back into the house muttering something in Spanish. Mom, after tending to my brother, went back to the kitchen and continued preparing lunch for the family. My sisters went back to their rooms to do whatever sisters do in their rooms. My brother returned to work on his motorcycle, and I returned to the pinball machine as the heat continued to rise on that eventful summer day in Texas, when I was a kid…

*(If you are wondering what happened to Patches, she ran out of gas ;-)*

# The Bosses

I T SEEMS LIKE I HAVE HAD LOTS OF BOSSES OVER MY LIFE. I recall the ones that taught me something. Probably the first job I had with a boss other than my dad was working at a U-Haul trailer and recreational vehicle rental business. The owner was Harold Smith, he was our next-door neighbor in San Antonio. He was originally a television repairman. He learned the trade in the Navy during World War II and operated three repair stores around the city. He sold that business, bought some land on a busy highway, and went into the trailer and recreational vehicle rental business. I did a lot of odd jobs including helping demolish several walls in his building and general cleanup. I learned how to wire a trailer, including splicing lines, replacing bulbs and cleaning the contacts really well and helped Ned install trailer hitches.

Ned was Mr. Smith's number one right-hand handy man. He was a big man with bushy uncontrolled red hair, a red uncontrolled beard, and huge uncontrolled wire brush like eyebrows he never trimmed. Ned could do anything he wanted to do. I think that was one of the problems with Ned, he only did what he wanted to. He gave me the other jobs, especially one's I had no experience with. I recall Ned asked me help to weld a broken iron stairway. We needed the stairs for a mobile-home Mr. Smith acquired. I had never seen a welder much less operated one. We grounded the welder cable to the stairway and put the rod into the other end that is somewhat shaped like a gun. I was to hold the rod on the metal object that was being welded and strike an electric arch with the metal. I started welding and Ned guided me.

When I burned the rod down to about two inches and made several puddles of metal blobs, Ned stopped me. He had to tap me on the shield. The shield protects you from any stray sparks of the molten metal and also had a dark plate of ultraviolet glass to protect your eyes from the arch flash. Ned told me it was worse than looking at the sun and not blinking for hour and can burn your corneas to a point of total blindness. I was scared. I was standing off to one side, backing up slowly as Ned explained how hot the metal could get when I placed my hand on the section of the stairways I just welded. I burned my arm, hand and fingers really bad. It was not a third degree burn but I had huge blisters that develop fast. It hurt like hell and Ned laughed. That's when I learned just how hot welded metal could be. I have always been careful around welding and hot metal since then. The burns eventually healed, but it took a while and I still have a faint scare. I learn a lot during the summer I work for Mr. Smith. As I reflect back on that job, I learned a lot at Mr. Smith's expense. Someone had to pay for all the stuff I either broke, lost or ruined. He was a kind man to put up with me and Ned and actually pay us.

My next boss was Terrel Joyner, the manager of the Cine Cinco Six Plex movie theater in Windsor Park Mall, in northeast San Antonio. It was the first theater in the city with six screens and nice soft cushioned chairs. I held that job all the way through high school. It was a good job, and I learned about the basic operations of a movie theater. Mr. Joyner let me count money with him and Tracy, one of the cashiers, after the last show of the evening started. I learned to count cash and often we would see five to twenty thousand dollars during a weekend run. He told me we always counted the money with three people in the room for safety reasons.

This was the first job I got fired from. All kinds of things went on behind the scenes. We were bad employees. I remember Mr. Joyner would leave for about two hours after we opened and go do something else. Tracy and I messed around a little, high school kid messing around. She was cute and fun. Anyways, several of my buddies including

Steve Enty, Mike Parker, Rusty Eppler, Ed Rodarte, Greg Alba, Joe Moon, Freddie Champion, Mike Love and a few others asked if I could sneak them into a movie the day before, during school. I think the show they wanted to see was "Slap Shot," a slap stick humor story about a bunch of misfit hockey players. Wanting to be cool, I figured I probably could sneak ten misfit, cheapskate, peer pressuring, adolescent idiot buddies in. I could time the scandal when Mr. Joyner left for his personal time. So, at the appointed time of 2:30pm, they showed up, went through the concession line, bought popcorn, cokes, candy, corndogs, Ice Slushies and headed down to me. I was taking tickets.

Little did I know we had a special visitor that day. Why would I know? I was not the manager. This guy, that I have never seen before is there and Mr. Joyner is gone. My buddies are all happy and walking down the stairs and I wave them though. Laughing and cutting up as they walk past. I made no effort to take a ticket. This guy, standing at the top of the stairs, leaning against the wall, is watching me. He springs into action and yells, "Hey! You can't let them in like that!" My buddies froze. They looked at me, I looked at them, we looked at the mystery guy. They all look back to me and I am speechless and frozen too. Our eyes were bouncing panicked glances back and forth like a scene from the standoff at the OK corral. The entire lobby was dead silent. Then the Steve Enty erupts and throws his popcorn and Coke high into the air. It goes flying everywhere. Then more popcorn and sodas go flying, my cheapskate buddies bolt like arch flashes to the exit door and vanish into the crowd in the mall. It was a Saturday, and the place was packed. The lobby is a disaster area. About that time, Mr. Joyner strolled back in. He turned beat red. He figured out what had happened really fast. I started to clean the lobby from the debris of popcorn, slushes, and sodas while the mystery man and Mr. Joyner headed upstairs to the office.

This guy, I don't remember his name, turned out to be the theater group area supervisor king pin. He was Mr. Joiners bosses' bosses, bosses, bosses, boss (remember this is a story about bosses) and lived on the west coast somewhere. After I cleaned up the mess and things started to settle down, Mr. Joyner called me into his office along with this other guy. He told me he had to fire me. Mr. Joyner explained that the mystery man did undercover surprise visits to the theaters under his purview in order to evaluate operations. He was pretty high up. He said I broke a cardinal rule of letting people into movies for free. He told me I should have asked for some passes and he would have given to me. Once I left the theater that afternoon, I knew I would have to face my parents. I didn't know what I would tell them, but I am sure they were going to be disappointed in me. I was disappointed in myself. I should have known better. I kept thinking my friends were all jerks but, I knew it was my fault.

I received a phone call from Mr. Joyner the next day. It was Sunday and he spoke to my father for a several minutes. Mr. Joyner re-hired me. He told me we all make mistakes and there are always a lot of opportunities to learn from our mistakes. He told me not to do it again and I didn't. He also said the chances of this area supervisor being around were really slim and he had never met this guy. I told him I knew I should not have done what I had done, and I was truly sorry. He said he understood. The man from the west coast asked Mr. Joiner to hire me back. I really respected Mr. Joyner and the other man for that. They were good men. One thing you should know about is that Mr. Joyner was a midget. He told me one time he just met the definition of four foot six inches to be considered an official midget. He was the coolest midget I ever met. He understood how show business worked and appreciated what to expect from kids. That was the year "Saturday Night Fever" with John Travolta came out. John Travolta visited our theater during the run of the movie. I got to meet him.

I ended up working for Mr. Joyner and the theater syndicate through the duration of my high school years. I started college the next fall and left the theater business for good, other than being a paying customer. I have a lot of respect for the people in the movie business. It was a fun job and I saw a lot of movies. I was able to get my family and friends in on passes occasionally.

I had several other jobs during the years after high school. I worked for Roto-Flex Oven Company, assisting in the installation of commercial ovens for pizza places and restaurants. I traveled around the country with that company. During my last two year of college, I participated in work-study programs and helped in the chemistry department. I learned about the storage and management of the lab supply rooms and dispensed chemicals for student laboratory experiments. But bosses I remember during this period changed frequently.

I enlisted into the military in 1983 and served honorably for 3 years. During this time, I was stationed at Ft. Hood Texas. I was assigned to the Sixty Fourth Engineering Detachment of the Third Corps. We were a small thirty-person engineering detachment and supported the 2nd Armored Division with terrain analysis and intelligence. Our commanding office was Captain Gustave Villarett III. He retired as a Lt. Col. And lives in El Paso, Texas. He is 91 years old. He was an interesting man and always supportive of those under his command. He drove a Rolls Royce, knew Latin and proffered bits of wisdom on three by five index note cards to the soldiers that needed his guidance and encouragement. One of the cards of wisdom I received from Captain Villarett involved the story of Apelles of Kos, a renowned painter of the fourth century B.C. The story referenced the correcting of a painted sandal. The comment came from some politician at the time who had no special knowledge of sandals, nor was a cobbler. Apelles retorted "One should not give judgement where one has no competence to judge." This was sound advice for a young soldier.

On two different occasions he selected me for temporary duty assignments in Europe. Our mission was to shadow a military exercise movement through the eastern border of Germany and photograph anything of interest. I recall we were supposed to pick-up four-wheel drive Audie cars at the Frankfurt International Airport, but the rental agency didn't have any, so they provided us with Mercedes 190e's to drive while in Europe taking pictures. I managed to get the car up to one-hundred-sixty-five kilometers per hour (102mph) on the autobahn. I liked that car. We were also instructed to NOT wear uniforms. We were to look like tourists.

This was during the Cold War and my real boss at the time was President Reagan, our Commander in Chief. For some unknown reason, our small detachment was picked to do this covert operation along the eastern German border near the Iron Curtain. Our orders stated to take photos of anything we thought looked interesting or important. I think most of the photos had pretty girls in them and the occasional castle. We did capture photos of demolition manholes scattered on roads and bridges. I took over twenty-five thousand photos during each mission. I learned how to use a Cannon AE-1 well.

After I my enlistment ended, I had several jobs, but the one I remember learning a lot from was the used car business. My boss was Fitz Saunders. I worked off and on with Fritz for probably eight years. I learned about buying cars and trucks at the San Antonio Auto Auction and how to flip them. Fitz sold so many cars and trucks it was unbelievable. He knew and worked pick-up and construction vehicle deals with national and international companies. That was how he made a good living. He drank a lot and helped me along that trail too. I recall one deal that went bad around the time we first met. It occurred as the result of the peso devaluation in 1982. Fitz was shipping a barge loaded with construction equipment to the Campeche Peninsula for the Mexican Government. The shipment included some Caterpillar Road graders and bulldozers and Ford flatbed construction trucks. He had over two million dollars invested in the cargo. He had a contract with a wealthy man name Mr. Elonis, a civil engineer from Mexico and in charge of the project for the government. He put down a thirty percent deposit for the equipment in pesos. The pesos were easily converted to dollars at the time.

The barge was on its way to Campeche and Fitz was on board the tugboat. It was a ten-day crossing of the Gulf of Mexico and a good vacation for him. He earned a few days off. He would make a nice little profit when the equipment landed. Eighty miles from the dock they heard on the ship's radio the value of the currency had plummeted. Overnight the peso became virtually worthless. They could not pay Fitz. He could not pay to ship the equipment back. It would have cost twenty thousand dollars he did not have. He was broke, but he wasn't down. He never declared bankruptcy. Fitz had his equipment impounded in one of the customs yards, made his way back to the United States and went into the battery re-building business. He eventually sold off the equipment piece by piece. Within five years, he would pay-off all his creditors, and have a little money in the bank. The battery business gave him cash in hand. It was his operating fund. I helped him with the battery business and getting it running. I learned how to help people with minor car issues. It mostly involved installing automotive batteries. If everything goes south, I know I'll always be able to start a battery business. Be good to the people you do business with, and they will be good to you is what I learned from Fitz. He knew and trusted lot of people and they trusted him. Fitz did what he said he would do, and he always met his obligations.

In 1990 I completed a B.A. in Geology. A few years later I started my career with the Department of Energy. I worked for the Federal Government for almost 30 years. My first boss was Jim Rasmussen. A GS-15 career employee. I was in the environmental compliance office along with about fourteen other staff. The Senior administrative staff rotated on about a four-year cycle that eerily resembled a pattern that coincides with the presidential election cycle. Faces changed depending on who was in office. I served under the following Presidents: Ronald Reagan for four years, Bill Clinton for eight years, George W. Bush for eight years, Barrack Obama for eight years, and Donald Trump for about four months. I received a very nice letter from the White House. The President and The First Lady wished me a successful retirement. It was suitable for framing. I have several stories about several bosses while in the Government. But that is another story.

# The Horse and
# The Saxophone

WHEN I WAS A KID, I WANTED A HORSE. NOT A PONY, BUT a horse. At seven years old, what kid didn't? We were living on Infantry Post, a subdivision for military officers and their families at Fort Sam Houston, Texas. I was an Army brat and we moved around a lot, so the logistics of owning a horse were difficult if not impossible. I see that now, but when you are seven years old all you hear is "No. Where would you keep it?" My mother tended to ask the most difficult questions. My dad didn't say much. I remember him telling me to go to the Boots and Saddle Club. This was a horse stable dedicated to the remnants of the last cavalry unit of the U.S. Army. There were lots of horses at the stables. I could ride one if I had a parent with me, but I wanted my own. One Christmas all that changed.

The hype of the 1966 Christmas season was bearing down on the family. Lyndon B. Johnson was President and Hubert Humphrey was his vice president. The Vietnam war was heating up. The whispered question around the house was "What should I get so and so?" and "Do you think they will like this or that?" All I remember is I really wanted a horse. I think I must have been persuasive and persistent. More like a nuisance in retrospect. I wrote a carefully worded letter to Santa asking for a saddle, saddle bags, a bridle, rope, bales of hay, and a bedroll to tie to the back of the saddle. I wanted to be a cavalry soldier and hero in the worst way. Just like in the movies, like John Wayne in "Fort Apache" and "Rio Grande" and the Lone Ranger. Of course, the most import thing a horse soldier or western hero can own is his horse. The closer and closer Christmas came, I was convinced I was going to get a horse. My parents dropped hints while I was around, by whispering things like "Do you think a twenty-foot rope is long enough?" "Did you find good boots?" and "Hey, did you find some hay?" I pretended to not hear the hints. A few packages with my name started to appear under the tree. But I ignored them, knowing something truly special was coming my way.

I remember I woke up early Christmas morning and flew down the stairs. No horse in the living room or kitchen. I ran down into the basement thinking ahh,

"Santa must have put him in the basement. That would be a great place to keep him." Nope. No horse. I looked out into the backyard think he may be tied up to the clothesline. I could not find him and started to realize there was a chance I wasn't going get a horse.

The rest of the family was stirring as I returned to the living room to survey the Christmas gifts scattered under the tree. My brother and sisters were sorting gifts. My dad was getting his coffee and mom was heating up tamales and smiling. We took turns opening our packages. I do recall receiving a "Magic Time Machine" made by the Mattel corporation. I asked for one of those too, just in case the horse didn't make it. As I opened other small gifts, I noted, no rope, saddle, bridle, or other horse hero related accouterments. I did get some socks. Once all the gifts were opened my dad looked at me and said, "Son, you have one more gift. It's out front."

My heart was pounding. I raced to the door swung it open and shot outside like a bullet. "Where is he? Where is he?" I gasped. "Don't see him!!" I was expecting to see a beautiful fifteen hand high, chestnut colored steed saddled and ready to ride. I frantically surveyed the yard and then looked up and down the street. I started to think he must have run off. "He's gone! He's run off!" I yelled.

"He's tied to the tree." Mom yelled back. I went back out the front door and sure enough, dangling from a low leafless branch, tied with a piece of frayed rope was a horse. A stick horse. It was a stick-horse with a plastic red and white cartoon head of a horse, a cheesy grin and yellow yarn for a mane. Horses don't really smile.

I was crushed, let down. My whole family was laughing. It was a good laugh at my expense. That was a mean joke. It has been a continuous thread of humor for my family over the years. It seems they bring it up around the holidays. Someone will ask "Hey, how's that horse of yours doing?" and snicker. It leads me to the rest of the story and drives me to ask, "When is a joke a good joke?"

My younger son Mateo took to music at an early age and after a year of learning the clarinet ended up playing an alto saxophone in his middle school jazz band. My wife and I committed to buy him a sax. He did some research and told us a good middle of the road sax was about $250.00. We thought that was a reasonable amount for a student's first real musical instrument. It was getting into the Christmas season, and I decide to play a joke on Mateo. I put a listing on Craigslist for an old, unplayable saxophone. I received a reply from a man in California. I explained it was for a practical joke. He wrote back saying he loved a good joke and sent the saxophone at his own expense. His name was Virgil. He was a cool guy.

The sax arrived and it was perfect. It was a small parlor sax from the early 1930's. It had seen much better days. It was horn was dented and bent and the nickel finish was well worn. Some of the keys were missing and there were no pads. It was in bad shape. Truth be told, it could never be played again. I packed it away. During the same period, my wife and I were looking for a real instrument. We found a nice Jupiter alto sax for around $200. It was a fair deal, with a case and several extras like a few new reeds, a neck strap and a music stand.

Christmas morning was set. As the boys woke up, I could hear the pounding of footsteps up and down the stairway. They came to our bedroom door, and excitedly told us Santa had come and presents were everywhere. We started down the stairs in robes and slippers. Carole walked into the kitchen to make coffee. The boys were viewing the spread of intriguing packages. Mateo picked up one of his gifts, the largest one. He knew what it was. It was the right shape and heft. He had a cheeky grin and he started to open the package. He carefully cut the tape with scissors. He pulled the tape off, then the wrapping paper to find newspaper and bubble wrappings. He then raised the sax out of the box. He was smiling, spun it around and at the same time I said "It's really a nice one. It just needs a little work."

"You and dad can hammer out the dents the shop." My wife told him. "The man we purchased it from said it was an antique and valuable. We will need to find a new mouthpiece, get some reeds from the music store and we will look for a case on Craigslist. It just needs a little oil too."

After a few minutes and a more thorough inspection, he was not smiling. I am not sure what he was thinking, but he displayed grace. He was grateful and thanked us.

He kept looking at the sax and we kept telling him it just needed a little work, and it would be fine for a beginning instrument. He carefully placed the sax back in the box. The expression of his face said, "you have got to be kidding."

We continued to open gifts. At one point, Carole headed to the kitchen to refresh our coffees. She asked Mateo to help. As he entered the kitchen, I heard him ask how much we paid for the sax. Whatever amount, it was way too much as far as he was concerned. As soon as he left the room, I switched out the old sax for the new Jupiter sax.

When he returned, I asked him to grab his sax so we could go to the shop and bang out some of the dents in the bell. I told him it needed some work and the sooner we worked on it, the sooner he would be able to play it. He was somewhat reluctant. But, as he reached for the box and opened it, his eyes lit up. He pulled the new sax out. He did not know what to say. He was confused and then elated and could not help smiling. He ended up playing it in the school jazz band. The saxophone became a pleasurable hobby for him. It was a good gift and a good practical joke.

I often wish I would have found a real horse tied to a tree Christmas 1966. I could have been a horse soldier or maybe the Lone Ranger and rode off into the sunset.

# She

SHE IS QUIETLY SLIPPING AWAY. IT STARTED AWHILE BACK; I just didn't want to admit it. Always the backbone of the family, it is difficult to watch. I wonder if it's dementia. Do we need a medical diagnosis to see the frail ninety-year-old woman is not the robust keenly sharp world traveler she once was? She was an Army wife and spent her young years hustling four kids to the next military outpost her husband was assigned to. She was the woman who could put together a five course Mexican feast for the Military lawyers and their wives with little notice. The woman who would sew her own clothing, mend ripped Levi's blue jeans and darn holes in socks worth mending. The mother who consoled her young daughter after breaking up with her first boyfriend. The woman who cheered her sons on the football field. And she kept her home cleaner than most others. She was a hailed as a beauty queen in the Charro Festival and could tango with a sultry swing of confidence.

When the doctor asks if she had any falls in the past year, she sheepishly looks him in the eye and shakes her head sideways, "No, doctor not that I can remember." In truth she has fallen eight times in the last year. Two were in a care facility. The other six in her home and in her yard. She loves tending her yard, the flowers, and tomatoes, and cucumber vines, and chili pequin plants. She loves gazing at the thirty-foot orange tree that started from a seed she spit out in her backyard twenty years ago. She reminds me she did not plant it on purpose. She loves the fresh semi-tart oranges but gives most away to her neighbors. She loves fresh fruits and veggies of all kinds. She will feed her birds in the morning and keep an eye out for her cat. A feral calico she calls "Sophie" that sticks close by. It's an unusual bond. She likes to cook for herself and others but that is becoming more difficult. She cooked the old fashion way, always using the freshest produce and meats, avoiding boxed products and items wrapped in plastic. She never truly liked plastic, it never felt right to her. She used to make her own flour tortillas. That stopped after an argument with her husband. Now she settles for store made tortilla. They are not that bad she says even though they come wrapped in plastic. She used to brag about being able to balance her check book to the penny. Now it takes five hours to review the five checks she wrote last month. She is incontinent and wears pads to help with the leaking. It is distracting and embarrassing for her. It would be for all of us. It is part of life now.

She was born in 1932, a child of the silent generation, a member of greatest generation, the mother to baby boomers, grandmother to the Millennials. She is a third-generation American citizen. She spoke, read, and wrote Spanish and English fluently. She never received a college degree, but she was smart. She knew how to fight, and how to argue. She spent more time in court rooms than most, fighting for her rights, and she won. She understood what was right and what was wrong. She grew up on the wrong side of the tracks in her town. She knew what discrimination was, but she never let those people stop her. She got out of that town and was able to travel. She liked to travel. She really enjoyed South America and Europe. She fell in love with the old cathedrals, and castles, and villages, and art. She liked oil paintings, still life mostly. She painted for a while, just as a hobby. She was quite good, but other priorities took time away from her passions. She does not do much now. It is getting more and more difficult. She had two strokes. She uses a cane sometimes and a walker nowadays. The Texas Department of Public Safety would not renew her driver's license even though she politely asked. She was always a good driver. Only one or two tickets in her life. No major accidents, just a fender bender once. Her eyes are clear. She had cataract surgery and sees as good as she ever will. She does not have arthritis like her brother David. He was bent over like a question mark. He died a few years ago. Her feet shuffle along quietly and slowly, but she is a tough one. We joke and laugh about taking better care of ourselves. "For this?" she chuckles. Her voice is still clear and crisp and if she wanted to, she could bark an order and it would happen. But she won't. Not anymore.

She does not use a computer. She handwrites letters and notes. She used to write to her brother Eleno a lot, but he died. I am always happy when I get a letter from her. I always answer her. I send her stories. She is my best fan and it's her unwritten rule, "Always answer those who have taken the time to write. It is the proper thing to do." Most of her friends are gone and those that are still alive are quiet. They don't call often, and she feels hesitant calling them, thinking they may not ever answer their phones again. The iPhone is challenging, too many buttons, too many apps, too many adds. The conversions are the same, "What's new with you?" she asks. "Nothing much, how about you?" she responds. The list of medical issues is sprinkled in the conversation, some news about the kids, and then the weather. Occasionally she will engage in a happy dialogue and find out about a friend's daughter who has another grandchild. She knows the feeling, she never thought she would be a grandmother to so many. She forgets their names.

It's winter now. She knows it. She wants to embrace it. She wants to feel alive and well and loved, until she can't. It's getting difficult. She likes it when she sleeps well. She likes deep rest. She is curious when her eyes open each day. "What am I going to do today?" she muses. She pulls her small feet from under the covers ever so slowly, thinking about her garden and flowers and tomatoes and Sophie. She swings gently to the edge of the high bed and then slides her small frail body over to meet the simple braided wool rug. She is up and shuffles to the bathroom in a rush looking at herself in the mirror and wondering, "Am I really that old?". Her tattooed eyebrows look perfect, they have for many years. She has taken good care of her teeth, slightly stained by her morning coffee. Then she will have her simple breakfast, a fried egg, a flour tortilla, a small banana and maybe some juice. Then she washes the dishes and shuffles off to remember what she has forgotten. She is quietly slipping away.